FINDING MOTHER

A JOURNEY OF LOSS AND LOVE

Student Workbook
Reading Comprehension
Character Education
Secondary Students

AN ANTHOLOGY OF THE
FINDING MOTHER SERIES
OF FOUR CHRONOLOGICAL MEMOIRS

Dr. Grace LaJoy Henderson

This Teacher's Guide <u>must</u> be used in conjunction with the Student Workbook for Finding Mother Series of four books or Finding Mother: A Journey of Loss and Love

FINDING MOTHER – STUDENT WORKBOOK
READING COMPREHENSION AND CHARACTER EDUCATION
Copyright ©2021 Grace LaJoy Henderson
Published by Inspirations by Grace LaJoy
Raymore, MO www.gracelajoy.com

ISBN: 978-1-7341868-8-8

All rights reserved. No portion of this book may be copied, reproduced or transmitted in any form without prior written permission from the publisher.

Printed in the United States of America

"Dr. Grace LaJoy's story needs to be an integral part of every secondary school and on every library bookshelf."
~Dr. Kerry C. Dixon, Educator

"My Finding Mother Series is a memorable keepsake, something that will go down in history."
~Dr. Grace LaJoy Henderson

TABLE OF CONTENTS

A Word from the Author   **Page 11**

Worksheets for Book One
Finding Mother After Five Decade: A Story of Hope

Lesson One
- Main Idea and Supporting Details
- Sequencing
- Literary Techniques: Flashback
- Identifying Cause and Effect
- Point of View
- Character Trait Discussion – *Empathetic*

Lesson Two
- Main Idea and Supporting Details
- Plot Analysis: Conflict
- Identifying Cause and Effect
- Context Clues
- Interpreting and Evaluating Information
- Character Trait Discussion – *Grateful*

Lesson Three
- Main Idea and Supporting Details
- Sequencing
- Plot Analysis: Conflict
- Identifying Cause and Effect
- Interpreting and Evaluating Information
- Character Trait Discussion – *Determined*

Lesson Four
- Main Idea and Supporting Details
- Sequencing
- Text Structure: Chronological Order
- Identifying Cause and Effect
- Interpreting and Evaluating Information
- Character Trait Discussion – *Tireless*

Lesson Five
- Main Idea and Supporting Details
- Sequencing
- Identifying Cause and Effect
- Interpreting and Evaluating Information
- Story Structure and Author Intention
- Character Trait Discussion – *Hopeful*

Lesson Six
- Main Idea and Supporting Details
- Sequencing
- Plot Analysis: Rising Action
- Identifying Cause and Effect
- Interpreting and Evaluating Information
- Character Trait Discussion – *Hopelessness*

Lesson Seven
- Main Idea and Supporting Details
- Plot Analysis: Climax
- Identifying Cause and Effect
- Interpreting and Evaluating Information
- Character Trait Discussion – *Euphoric*

Worksheets for Book Two
After the Reunion: A Story of Acceptance

Lesson One
- Main Idea and Supporting Details
- Sequencing
- Plot Analysis
- Identifying Cause and Effect
- Textual Evidence
- Point of View
- Character Trait Discussion – *Zealous*

Lesson Two
- Main Idea and Supporting Details
- Sequencing
- Themes: Expectation Vs. Reality
- Literary Techniques: Emotive Language
- Identifying Cause and Effect
- Textual Evidence
- Character Trait Discussion: *Sedulous*

Lesson Three
- Main Idea and Supporting Details
- Sequencing
- Literary Technique: Descriptive Language
- Literary Elements: Mood
- Identifying Cause and Effect
- Textual Evidence
- Character Trait Discussion – *Open-minded*

Lesson Four
- Main Idea and Supporting Details
- Sequencing
- Plot Analysis: Falling Action
- Identifying Cause and Effect
- Character Transformation
- Character Trait Discussion – *Patient*

Lesson Five
- Main Idea and Supporting Details
- Plot Analysis: Resolution
- Identifying Cause and Effect
- Textual Evidence
- Author's Intention
- Story Summary
- Character Trait Discussion – *Tenaciousness*

Worksheets for Book Three
Reuniting with Mother: A Story of Tenacity

Lesson One
- Main Idea and Supporting Details
- Sequencing
- Plot Analysis
- Point of View
- Identifying Cause and Effect
- Comparing and Contrasting
- Character Analysis
- Contextual Meaning
- Character Trait Discussion – *Benevolent*

Lesson Two
- Main Idea and Supporting Details
- Sequencing
- Point of Vies
- Genre
- Author's Purpose
- Identifying Cause and Effect
- Comparing and Contrasting
- Interpreting and Evaluating Information
- Character Trait Evidence
- Contextual Meaning
- Character Trait Discussion – *Thoughtful*

Lesson Three
- Main Idea and Supporting Details
- Sequencing
- Author's Purpose
- Identifying Cause and Effect
- Interpreting and Evaluating Information
- Contextual Meaning
- Character Analysis
- Character Trait Discussion – *Altruistic*

Lesson Four
- Main Idea and Supporting Details
- Sequencing
- Author's Purpose
- Identifying Cause and Effect
- Interpreting and Evaluating Information
- Comparing and Contrasting
- Language: Idioms
- Inference
- Character Analysis
- Character Trait Discussion – *Loving*

Lesson Five
- Main Idea and Supporting Details
- Sequencing
- Author's Purpose
- Identifying Cause and Effect
- Literary Techniques: Descriptive Language
- Character Analysis
- Character Trait Discussion – *Accommodating*

Lesson Six
- Main Idea and Supporting Details
- Character Analysis: Geneva
- Identifying Cause and Effect
- Interpreting and Evaluating Information
- Contetual Meaning
- Character Trait Discussion – *Acquiescent*

Lesson Seven
- Main Idea and Supporting Details
- Literary Devices: Flashback
- Literary Elements: Tone
- Identifying Cause and Effect
- Contextual Meaning
- Inference
- Character Trait Discussion – *Affable*

Worksheets for Book Three
Reuniting with Mother: A Story of Tenacity Continued...

Lesson Eight
- Main Idea and Supporting Details
- Character Analysis
- Identifying Cause and Effect
- Interpreting and Evaluating Information
- Comparing and Contrasting
- Character Trait Discussion – *Enthusiastic*

Lesson Nine
- Main Idea and Supporting Details
- Summarizing
- Point of Vies
- Identifying Cause and Effect
- Interpreting and Evaluating Information
- Character Trait Analysis: Geneva
- Character Trait Discussion – *Appreciation*

Lesson Ten
- Main Idea and Supporting Details
- Story Elements: Dialogue
- Identifying Cause and Effect
- Reading for Information
- Contextual Meaning
- Character Trait Discussion – *Understanding*

Lesson Eleven
- Main Idea and Supporting Details
- Sequencing
- Character Analysis
- Literary Elements: Theme
- Identifying Cause and Effect
- Interpreting and Evaluating Information
- Character Trait Discussion – *Inquisitive*

Lesson Twelve
- Main Idea and Supporting Details
- Sequencing
- Literary Elements: Theme
- Figurative Language: Symbolism
- Inference
- Character Analysis
- Comparing and Contrasting
- Character Trait Discussion – *Accepting*

Worksheets for Book Four
Diary of Emotions: Thoughts and Feelings

Lesson One
- Main Idea and Supporting Details
- Plot Analysis: Internal Conflict
- Analyzing Characters and Incidents
- Identifying Cause and Effect
- Drawing Conclusions
- Character Trait Discussion – *Forgiving*

Lesson Two
- Main Idea and Supporting Details
- Point of View: Objective vs. Subjective Narrator
- Making Inferences
- Analyzing Characters and Incidents
- Identifying Cause and Effect
- Character Trait Discussion – *Understanding*

Lesson Three
- Main Idea and Supporting Details
- Literary Elements: Theme
- Character Analysis
- Identifying Cause and Effect
- Reading for Information
- Character Trait Discussion – *Acceptance*

Lesson Four
- Main Idea and Supporting Details
- Literary Elements: Theme
- Literary Techniques
- Identifying Cause and Effect
- Reading for Information
- Character Trait Discussion – *Curiosity*

Lesson Five
- Main Idea and Supporting Details
- Literary Elements: Tone
- Identifying Cause and Effect
- Interpreting and Evaluating Information
- Character Trait Discussion – *Adaptable*

Lesson Six
- Main Idea and Supporting Details
- Literary Elements: Style
- Identifying Cause and Effect
- Interpreting and Evaluating Information
- Character Trait Discussion – *Compassionate*

Lesson Seven
- Main Idea and Supporting Details
- Author's Purpose
- Identifying Cause and Effect
- Interpreting and Evaluating Information
- Character Trait Discussion – *Generous*

Lesson Eight
- Main Idea and Supporting Details
- Character Analysis
- Identifying Cause and Effect
- Interpreting and Evaluating Information
- Comparing and Contrasting
- Character Trait Discussion – *Sensible*

Lesson Nine
- Main Idea and Supporting Details
- Making Inferences
- Character Analysis
- Identifying Cause and Effect
- Character Trait Discussion – *Unprejudiced*

Lesson Ten
- Main Idea and Supporting Details
- Reading for Information
- Identifying Cause and Effect
- Character Trait Discussion – *Talented*

Worksheets for Book Four
Diary of Emotions: Thoughts and Feelings Continued...

Lesson Eleven
- Main Idea and Supporting Details
- Making Inferences
- Character Trait Discussion – *Perceptive*

Lesson Twelve
- Main Idea and Supporting Details
- Making Inferences
- Identifying Cause and Effect
- Character Decisions and Actions
- Character Trait Discussion – *Dutiful*

Lesson Thirteen
- Main Idea and Supporting Details
- Reading for Information
- Identifying Cause and Effect
- Interpreting and Evaluating Information
- Character Trait Discussion – *Magnanimous*

Lesson Fourteen
- Main Idea and Supporting Details
- Interpreting and Evaluating Information
- Character Trait Discussion – *Introspective*

Lesson Fifteen
- Main Idea and Supporting Details
- Making Inferences
- Reading for Information
- Identifying Cause and Effect
- Character Trait Discussion – *Rational*

Lesson Sixteen
- Main Idea and Supporting Details
- Character Decisions and Actions
- Character Trait Discussion – *Optimistic*

Lesson Seventeen
- Main Idea and Supporting Details
- Making Inferences
- Reading for Information
- Character Trait Discussion – *Practical*

Lesson Eighteen
- Main Idea and Supporting Details
- Making Inferences
- Character Trait Discussion – *Undecided*

Lesson Nineteen
- Main Idea and Supporting Details
- Reading for Information
- Interpreting and Inferring
- Character Trait Discussion – *Responsible*

Lesson Twenty
- Main Idea and Supporting Details
- Reading for Information
- Interpreting and Evaluating Information
- Character Trait Discussion – *Self-Reliant*

Lesson Twenty-One
- Main Idea and Supporting Details
- Character Decisions and Actions
- Identifying Cause and Effect
- Character Trait Discussion – *Thoughtful*

Lesson Twenty-Two
- Main Idea and Supporting Details
- Making Predictions
- Character Trait Discussion – *Capable*

Lesson Twenty-Three
- Main Idea and Supporting Details
- Making Predictions
- Identifying Cause and Effect
- Character Trait Discussion – *Giving*

Worksheets for Book Four
Diary of Emotions: Thoughts and Feelings Continued...

Lesson Twenty-Four
- Main Idea and Supporting Details
- Identifying Cause and Effect
- Character Trait Discussion – *Initiator*

Lesson Twenty-Five
- Main Idea and Supporting Details
- Interpreting and Evaluating Information
- Character Trait Discussion – *Complaisant*

Lesson Twenty-Six
- Main Idea and Supporting Details
- Textual Evidence
- Character Trait Discussion – *Respectfulness*

Lesson Twenty-Seven
- Main Idea and Supporting Details
- Analyzing Character
- Making Inferences and Drawing Conclusions
- Character Trait Discussion – *Appreciative*

Lesson Twenty-Eight
- Main Idea and Supporting Details
- Making Inferences and Drawing Conclusions
- Identifying Cause and Effect
- Character Trait Discussion – *Considerate*

Lesson Twenty-Nine
- Main Idea and Supporting Details
- Reading for Information
- Analyzing Dialogue
- Identifying Cause and Effect
- Character Trait Discussion – *Supportive*

Lesson Thirty
- Main Idea and Supporting Details
- Reading for Information
- Character Decisions and Actions
- Interpreting and Evaluating Information
- Character Trait Discussion – *Charitable*

A Word from the Author

Hello, my name is Dr. Grace LaJoy Henderson, author of over 35 books.

Studies have shown when young people go through challenging situations, they often lack the skills of how to use their stories in a way that empower themselves and others. They can't see into the future to see how their life will turn out.

But, with my Finding Mother Series, they get a glimpse of what life can look like after going through various life circumstances. They will realize that it is the exact circumstance, that they are going through at this very moment, that is giving them the lemons they need to make lemonade.

They will also learn that they are not alone in many of the natural emotions, thoughts and feelings they experience. Not to mention, that some of our children may share my *exact* situation of living without their mother in their lives.

At only two years old, my mother left my siblings and I with our father whose unviability led me down a path where I experienced numerous challenges from living in foster care to becoming a teen mom.

When I wrote my foster care story, A Gifted Child in Foster Care: A Story of Resilience in 2009, I had no idea I would ever find my mother. She had been gone for 41 years when I wrote the story, so finding her seemed to be only a dream that would never, ever come true. Later, when I knew she would be around 80 years old, I gave up all hope of ever finding her alive.

But, on March 2, 2018, I found my mother after 49 years!

And I share the entire story in my Finding Mother Series.

After I completed the Finding Mother Series, I received feedback from readers. It turned out there were a lot of people who were inspired because they, too, had been trying to find a long-lost loved one with no success. My story gave them hope.

When I was growing up, with all of the other feelings that went along with my circumstances, I had no idea my story would have a positive effect on so many people. When the Sherriff removed me from a house, where my father left me and my siblings, with no food or utilities, I had no idea I would one day be writing my foster care story. When I wrote my finding mother story, I had no idea I would end up creating the Anthology, let alone creating matching workbooks, to enhance reading comprehension and character education for middle and high school students.

Our students represent the youngest branch of society but that doesn't mean they don't experience life-changing challenges. That's where my story com

es in. When students experience my story, they will know that their lives, regardless of their circumstances, can be a blessing to others.

My story reveals how a foster child becomes an author and finds her mother after 49 years of separation. My finding mother series teaches students that they have the power to overcome any challenge in life; and that their challenges can be used to benefit others. Put this book in the hands of your students and watch them put my theories of self-development into practice as they realize the power of their own stories.

Book 1

Finding Mother

Answer Keys
Chapters 1-7

Lesson One - Worksheet

This lesson coincides with Chapter 1 of the book, 'Finding Mother'. The purpose of this lesson is to analyze the reason for the main character's problem using key points from the text.
Chapter One – "Before Mother Left"

Main Idea and Supporting Details

Place an X on the line beside the main idea of the text.

_____ The author's father physically harmed her mother.

_____ The author's mother was mentally unfit to care for her family.

_____ The author empathized with her father because he cared for her.

The <u>four</u> *statements below "support" the main idea. Fill in the blanks with the correct word.*

(a) Mother would often experience _____, which resulted in the harming of the author and her siblings.

(b) Jerome told the author that their _____ is not to be blamed for their mother's condition.

(c) Father experienced a lot of _____ and _____ due to his wife having a mental illness.

(d) Father did not receive the _____ he desired from his wife.

Sequencing

Rearrange the following lines from Chapter 1 by numbering them correctly.

(   ) The author blamed her father for her mother's emotional state.

(   ) The author has some very heartbreaking memories of her mother.

(   ) Father was disappointed due to his wife having a mental illness.

(   ) Mother left when the author was only two years old.

(   ) Father had called the authorities to take mother to a mental hospital.

(   ) The author remembers her mother beating her with a broomstick once.

Literary Techniques: Flashback

Using flashbacks as a story device, the author takes readers back in time to explain something that happened. Answer the following questions in a word or more.

(a) Which year or decade is the author recalling events from? _____

(b) How old was the author during that time? _____

Identifying Cause and Effect

"I heard stories about my mother's mental illness causing her to experience episodes, which resulted in her harming my siblings and me."

What is the Cause? _____

What is the Effect? _____

Point of View

'Point of view' means the position from which something or someone is observed.

'First Person' is when the story is told from the point of view of a character. *E.g. I, we, me, us*

'Second Person' is when the narrator talks to the reader. *E.g. you, yours*

'Third Person' is when the narrator is not a part of the story. *E.g. he, she, it*

(a) Who is telling the story in Chapter 1? _____

(b) Circle the narrator's point of view in Chapter 1:   First   Second   Third

Character Trait Discussion

The character trait for Chapter 1 is "empathetic".

Empathetic means showing the ability to understand and share the feelings of another.

Read the statement below. Then choose one of the questions below and answer it. Write your answer in the space provided then discuss it with your group.

The author has expressed sorrow for her mother's predicament in the story. She even says that her mother did not deserve any abuse from her father.

1. Would you feel empathy if someone you loved was treated badly? Explain why or why not.

2. Describe a situation where you felt empathetic towards someone or something.

3. Do you think it is important to show empathy to those who are going through something difficult? Explain and include an example if possible.

Lesson Two - Worksheet

This lesson coincides with Chapter 2 of the book, 'Finding Mother'. The purpose of this lesson is to analyze the feelings of the main character after a specific event.
Chapter Two – "After Mother Left"

Main Idea and Supporting Details

Place an "X" on the line beside the main idea of Chapter 2.

_____ The author misses her mother and wants to find her.

_____ The author feels bad about her own mother not wanting to receive her.

_____ The author's father is sensible and genuinely cares about his family.

The <u>four</u> statements below "support" the main idea. Fill in the blanks with the correct word.

(a) The protagonist did not _____ with what her father said about her mother.

(b) The protagonist felt that her grandmother and father were just making excuses

because they _____ her mother.

(c) The protagonist felt _____ to tell her father that she wanted to find her

mother.

(d) Wanting to know her mother's side of the story, _____ the author to find her.

Plot Analysis: Conflict

The conflict in a story is the struggle faced by two opposing forces. It is usually the main character that faces some sort of conflict, either with another character (person vs. person) or with themselves (person vs. self).

In 'Finding Mother', the author does not believe her father's reasons for her mother leaving and rejecting her. Although she misses her mother terribly, the author is hesitant to tell her father that she wants to find her.

What kind of conflict do you think the author is facing here? Circle the letter for the correct answer.

a) Person vs. Person   b) Person vs. Self   c) Both

Identifying Cause and Effect

"My father often complained about how my mother got a job working for a dry cleaner and was terminated when she refused to do things according to her boss's instructions."

What is the cause? _____

What is the effect? _____

Context Clues

Read the following line from the story, and figure out the meaning of the highlighted word using clues in the sentence. Circle the letter for the correct answer once you are sure.

He **mocked** her voice as he reminisced about the way she used to say, "One of these days I'm going to go far, far away."

a) insulted

b) made fun of

c) imitated

Interpreting and Evaluating Information

How does the author truly feel about the things her father said about her mother? Write three things from Chapter 2.

1. _____

2. _____

3. _____

Character Trait Discussion

The character trait for Chapter 2 is "grateful".

Grateful means feeling or showing an appreciation for something done or received.

Read the statement below. Then choose <u>one</u> of the questions below and answer it. Write your answer in the space provided then discuss it with your group.

In the story, the author said she felt grateful that her mother left to get the break she needed.

1. Name one or more things a person may do when they are feeling grateful. Provide one or more examples for each thing you name.

2. What is something that you are extremely grateful for right now?

3. How would you teach someone to be grateful?

_____
_____
_____
_____
_____
_____
_____
_____
_____
_____
_____

Lesson Three - Worksheet

This lesson coincides with Chapter 3 of the book, 'Finding Mother'. The purpose of this lesson is to understand the difficulties faced by the main character in achieving her goal.
Chapter Three – "The Search"

Main Idea and Supporting Details

Place an "X" on the line beside the main idea of the text.

_____ Grace uses many online and offline resources to locate her mother.

_____ Grace is hoping that her mother will respond to her letters.

_____ Grace keeps trying hard to find her mother though her efforts are in vain.

The <u>four</u> statements below "support" the main idea. Fill in the blanks with the correct word.

(a) Grace wanted to find her mother even though she was afraid of being _____.

(b) Grace requested for the marriage license and application for her parents

from the _____.

(c) Grace could not wait to search for her mother using her _____

and her _____.

(d) Grace sent a letter to four women named _____, hoping that one of

them would be her mother.

Sequencing

Following the timeline of Grace's search techniques in Chapter 3, rearrange the following events in the correct order.

(   ) She then used online white pages to search for addresses and phone numbers.

(   ) She later visited a couple of Genealogical Research Libraries.

(   ) Grace went to the local Social Security Administration office to ask them for help.

(   ) Then she contacted an online people locator service.

(   ) Finally, she sent out a letter to four women who shared her mother's name.

(   ) She asked for her parents' marriage license from the State Dept. of Public Health.

Plot Analysis: Conflict

The central conflict is the main problem in a story. The conflict makes a story interesting to read and shows the motivations of the characters, as well as the consequences of their actions. Chapter 1 and 2 of 'Finding Mother' introduced us to Grace's family with some background information. What is the main conflict for Grace in Chapter 3?

_____
_____
_____
_____
_____
_____

Identifying Cause and Effect

"I was disappointed in her as I felt like she did not care what happened to the twin boys."

What is the cause? _____

What is the effect? _____

Interpreting and Evaluating Information

Why did the excitement of finding her mother start to dwindle for Grace?
Circle the letter for the correct answer.

a) None of her search attempts was successful.

b) The Calvin she spoke to was not the one she was looking for.

c) None of the four women she wrote to was her mother.

d) All of the above.

Character Trait Discussion

The character trait for Chapter 3 is "determined".

Determined means having made a firm decision and being resolved not to change it.

Read the statement below. Then choose one of the questions below and answer it. Write your answer in the space provided then discuss it with your group.

In Chapter 3, we see how determined Grace is to find her mother through all her search attempts and techniques.

1. Describe a time when you felt determined to achieve something?

2. Do you know someone who has great determination in life? If so, who? What has this person done to show that they have determination?

3. Why do you think that it is good to be determined? Name at least one advantage or disadvantage to being determined?

_____

_____

_____

_____

_____

_____

_____

_____

_____

_____

Lesson Four - Worksheet

This lesson coincides with Chapter 4 of the book, 'Finding Mother'. The purpose of this lesson is to analyze some information that adds more significance to the plot.
Chapter Four – "The Search Continues"

Main Idea and Supporting Details

Place an "X" on the line beside the main idea of the text.

_____ Grace is still unable to find her mother despite several searches.

_____ Grace discovers some new information about her birth and her mother.

_____ Grace's brother had kept their parents' divorce order for many years.

The <u>four</u> statements below "support" the main idea. Fill in the blanks with the correct word.

(a) Grace's birth records showed that her _____ took her home from the hospital.

(b) Grace wondered if _____ could be her sibling.

(c) Geneva's birth certificate listed Grace's _____ as her birth mother.

(d) Geneva's original name was _____.

Sequencing

Say whether the following statements are true or false. Write "T" for true and "F" for false.

(a) Grace's mother had left her in Kansas City.   _____

(b) The "state hospital" mentioned in Grace's birth records was a normal hospital.   _____

(c) Kevin was born in the 1930s.   _____

(d) Joe was Geneva's actual birth father.   _____

(e) Grace did not know that her brother had their parents' divorce order.   _____

(f) Grace was five years old when her parents divorced.   _____

Text Structure: Chronological Order

Authors sometimes write stories using the chronological order structure. In the chronological structure, the events in the story are told in the order they happened. It is also called "time order."

In chapter 4, the author takes us through her journey of searching for her mother by using dates to mark what happened.

Write one-line answers to say what happened in the story on the following dates.

(a) January 10, 1998 – _____
_____
_____

(b) May 4, 1998 – _____
_____

(c) September 11, 2008 – _____
_____

Identifying Cause and Effect

"I presumed that she did not necessarily "leave" those children in the hospital, but was unable to take them home due to being in a mental hospital at the time of their births, causing the babies to become automatic wards of the state."

What is the cause? _____

What is the effect? _____
_____

Interpreting and Evaluating Information

Do you think Grace became more appreciative of her father at the end of the chapter?

Circle the letter for the correct answer.

a) No, she still thinks her father is responsible for her mother leaving.

b) Yes, because she felt like her father truly wanted her and it gave her security.

c) No, although she is ambivalent about both her parents.

Character Trait Discussion

The character trait for Chapter 4 is "tireless".

Tireless means having or showing great effort or energy.

Read the statement below. Then choose one of the questions below and answer it. Write your answer in the space provided then discuss it with your group.

In Chapter 4, Grace shows how tireless she is in continuing to search for her mother. Only after many attempts does she give up to take a break.

1. Do you think that Grace should have just given up the search for her mother at that point? Explain why or why not.

2. What is something that you would work tirelessly for?

3. Write about a time when you did not give up? What was the result?

_____

_____

_____

_____

_____

_____

_____

_____

_____

_____

Lesson Five - Worksheet

> This lesson coincides with Chapter 5 of the book, 'Finding Mother'. The purpose of this lesson is to understand the main character's motivation behind pursuing her goal.
> **Chapter Five – "The Search Continues"**

Main Idea and Supporting Details

Place an "X" on the line beside the main idea of the text.

_____ Grace is hopeful about finding her mother even though it's been forty-one years.

_____ Some kind-hearted people have come forward to help Grace find her mother.

_____ Grace has already tried to find her mother using her social security number.

The four statements below "support" the main idea. Fill in the blanks with the correct word.

(a) Grace walked into a _____ office to help her find her mother.

(b) Grace decided to use the _____ for her new book to try to locate her mother.

(c) When she published her foster care story, Grace purposely included the names of her _____ and _____.

(d) Grace sent a _____ with _____ to her mother through the Social Security Administration Office.

Sequencing

"X" all the things that Grace did in Chapter 5 to search for her mother.

Grace searched for Geneva's biological family.	( )
She paid Sherry to help her find Geneva.	( )
She decided to use the announcement for her new book to try to locate her mother.	( )
Using the address the woman found for her, Grace visited the property.	( )
She included the real names of her family in her foster care story hoping that someone would recognize it.	( )
Grace went on the TV show even though they couldn't find her mother.	( )

Identifying Cause and Effect

"However, due to Joe having such a common first and last name, there were tons of them listed in the census records. As a result, it was impossible to tell which one of them was the correct one."

What is the cause? _____
_____

What is the effect? _____
_____

Interpreting and Evaluating Information

How did Grace feel when some people volunteered to help her find her mother?
Circle the letter for the correct answer.

a) She felt that they would not be successful, but was willing to give them a chance.

b) She did not feel confident that they would come up with anything.

c) She was certain that they would be able to find her mother using her social security number.

Story Structure and Author Intention

Writers structure stories in different ways, depending on their reasons for writing them.

A **milieu** story structure focuses on the world surrounding the characters you create.

A **character** story structure is all about the character's growth, transformation or downfall.

An **event** story structure is about fixing an external problem where something is wrong and the characters need to set it right.

What structure is the author following for 'Finding Mother'?

Circle the letter for the correct answer.

(a) milieu   (b) character   (c) event

Character Trait Discussion

The character trait for Chapter 4 is "hopeful".
Hopeful means feeling or inspiring optimism about a future event.

Read the statement below. Then choose one of the questions below and answer it. Write your answer in the space provided then discuss it with your group.

In this chapter, Grace tries to remain hopeful about finding her mother one day despite several unsuccessful attempts to locate her.

1. Do you think it is good to be hopeful for things? Explain why or why not.

2. What is something you have been hopeful for something? Did you receive what you were hoping for?

3. What do you think is the right way to handle disappointment?

_____

_____

_____

_____

_____

_____

_____

_____

_____

_____

_____

Lesson Six - Worksheet

This lesson coincides with Chapter 6 of the book, 'Finding Mother'. The purpose of this lesson is to understand the impact of failure on the main character and how she deals with it.
Chapter Six – "Losing Hope, Then Finding a Glimmer"

Main Idea and Supporting Details

Place an "X" on the line beside the main idea of the text.

_____ Grace feels like nobody can help her find her mother.

_____ Grace has almost given up hope on finding her mother.

_____ Grace imagined miraculously finding her mother though hope was dim.

The four statements below "support" the main idea. Fill in the blanks with the correct word.

(a) Grace felt _____ when the talk shows she wrote to did not respond to her messages.

(b) Instead of feeling _____, she was beginning to feel _____.

(c) Grace decided that if she could not find her mother, she would try to locate her

   _____.

(d) Grace felt good that she found _____ related to her mother in some way.

Sequencing
Write YES or NO as the answer for each statement.

(a) Grace lost hope in finding her mother during her inactive searching time. _____

(b) She felt annoyed when the suggestions people gave her didn't work out. _____

(c) Grace never enjoyed watching TV talk show reunions. _____

(d) She felt happy for the people who had found their relatives even though she hadn't found hers. _____

(e) Grace decided to watch the reunion show immediately after her friend told her about it. _____

(f) Grace's big sister Carla had been missing for over ten years. _____

Plot Analysis: Rising Action

The rising action in a story moves the plot closer to the climax. It is the part where obstacles stand in the way of the author achieving his/her goal.

What obstacle do you think Grace has to get through in order to achieve her goal of finding her mother?

(a) Facing the reality of perhaps never finding her at all.

(b) Dealing with endless searches, which could take years to produce any strong leads.

(c) Not being able to find a single clue about her mother's whereabouts.

(d) All of the above.

Identifying Cause and Effect

"Because of my increasingly raw feelings, I eventually stopped watching reunion shows altogether. I purposely avoided those types of shows because they revealed the harsh reality that my mother was missing and I may never find her."

What is the cause? _____

_____

What is the effect? _____

_____

Interpreting and Evaluating Information

Circle the letter for the correct answer.

From the feelings expressed by the author in this chapter, we can conclude that....

a) She feels frustrated and hopeless about ever finding her mother.

b) She is jealous of the people on talk show reunions because they could find their relatives.

c) She has not completely given up as she has decided to look for her siblings and mother's relatives.

(d) All of the above.

Character Trait Discussion

The character trait for Chapter 4 is "hopelessness".
Hopelessness means a feeling or state of despair.

Read the statement below. Then choose one of the questions below and answer it.
Write your answer in the space provided then discuss it with your group.

In this chapter, Grace is beginning to feel completely hopeless and has started feeling jealous of people who have found their long-lost family members.

1. When would you give up if you were searching for a missing relative?
2. Discuss a time when you completely lost hope in something?
3. How would you encourage someone who has lost hope in something they wanted so badly?

_____

_____

_____

_____

Lesson Seven - Worksheet

This lesson coincides with Chapter 7 of the book, 'Finding Mother'. The purpose of this lesson is to analyze the techniques used by the main character to achieve her goal.
Chapter Seven – "I Found My Mother!"

Main Idea and Supporting Details

Place an "X" on the line beside the main idea of the text.

_____ Grace was about to cease searching for her mother after one last attempt.

_____ Grace could not believe that she was able to talk to her mother.

_____ Grace is overjoyed about finding her mother after almost 50 years.

The <u>four</u> statements below "support" the main idea. Fill in the blanks with the correct word.

(a) Grace's mother Geneva, was residing at a _____.

(b) A woman named _____ helped Grace to connect with her mother.

(c) Grace felt _____ about why Geneva asked her who she was after answering all of her questions.

(d) Grace immediately informed her brother _____ about finding their mother.

Plot Analysis: Climax

The climax is the highest point of interest in a story. This is where the conflict is at the highest point of tension.

It was an anxious moment for Grace when she was trying to confirm if she had actually found her mother. She feels nervous while talking to Geneva on the phone hoping that she was indeed her long-lost mother.

Describe how this part of the story made you feel before and after Grace spoke to Geneva.

_____

_____

_____

_____

Identifying Cause and Effect

"I explained to her that she was in a different state and I was in Missouri, so I could not just come right over. But, that I would come as soon as I possibly could."

What is the Cause? _____

What is the Effect? _____

Interpreting and Evaluating Information
Circle the letter for correct answer for the two questions below.

What information did Grace use to finally locate her mother?
a) her name and date of birth

b) her name, date of birth and state

c) her name and social security number

Apart from this information, what prediction about her mother did Grace get right?

a) Her mother was immobile and lying in bed in a mental hospital.

b) Her mother could not remember her or her siblings.

c) Her mother was eighty-something years old.

Character Trait Discussion
The character trait for Chapter 4 is "euphoric".
Euphoric means feeling intense excitement and happiness.

*Read the statement below. Then choose <u>one</u> of the questions below and answer it.
Write your answer in the space provided then discuss it with your group.*

In Chapter 7, Grace has finally accomplished finding her mother after 50 years, and she feels euphoric about it.

1. Write about an incident that made you feel euphoric about something.

2. How would you feel if your friend received a reward and you did not?

3. Give some examples of situations where one should feel euphoric.

_____

_____

Book 2

Reuniting with Mother

Answer Keys
Chapters 1-5

Lesson One – Worksheet

> This lesson coincides with Chapter 1 of the book, 'Reuniting with Mother'. The purpose of this lesson is to understand the emotions of the characters in the story, because of an important event. **Chapter One – "After Finding Mother"**

Main Idea and Supporting Details
Place an X on the line beside the main idea of the text.

_____ Grace and her brothers were not sure if their mother would receive them.

_____ Grace's brothers did not want her to drive to her mother's destination.

_____ Grace was eager to see her mother as soon as possible.

The <u>four</u> statements below "support" the main idea. Fill in the blanks with the correct word.

(a) Grace had waited _____ years to see her mother and could not wait any longer.

(b) Terrance warned Grace of a _____ in the area where their mother lives.

(c) Grace's _____ paid for all her expenses so that she could travel to see her mother.

(d) Jerome suggested that they leave on _____ and return on _____.

Sequencing
Rearrange the following lines from Chapter 1 by numbering them correctly.

( ) The following morning, Grace drove to Terrence's house to go to the airport with him.

( ) Grace receives an email from the private investigator she contacted a few days ago.

( ) After landing, they ate some food and boarded the connecting flight to their mother.

( ) The next morning, Jerome suggested the dates when they could leave and return.

( ) Grace informed Terrence, and Jerome informed Grayson about their mother.

( ) They then boarded the flight departing from Kansas City to a connecting flight.

Plot Analysis: Exposition

The exposition is the beginning of the story where the characters and setting are introduced. Complete the box below with details of the exposition in Chapter 1.

Exposition

a. Setting:

b. Time:

c. Main character's name:

d. Secondary characters:

e. Mood:

f. Point of view:

Identifying Cause and Effect

"Excited about me finally finding my mother, my daughter paid all my expenses to reunite with her, which included my plane ticket."

What is the cause? _____

What is the Effect? _____

Textual Evidence

Cite two lines from the text to show that Grace was nervous about visiting her mother. Explain why you picked those lines in the second box.

Textual Evidence	Explanation
1. 2.	

43

The character trait for Chapter 1 is "zealous".
Zealous means showing great enthusiasm for a cause or objective.

Read the statement below. Then choose one of the questions below and answer it. Write your answer in the space provided then discuss it with your group.

In this chapter, Graces says that she feels zealous about finally getting to see her mother again.

1. Would you feel zealous about meeting a long lost relative after many years? What would you do when you finally meet them?

2. What are some things that would make you zealous?

3. Do you think it is good to be zealous? Why or why not?

_____
_____
_____
_____
_____
_____
_____
_____
_____
_____
_____
_____
_____
_____

Lesson Two - Worksheet

This lesson coincides with Chapter 2 of the book, 'Reuniting with Mother'. The purpose of this lesson is to understand the negative feelings of the characters after an unexpected outcome.
Chapter Two – "Seeing Mother After 49 Years"

Main Idea and Supporting Details
Place an X on the line beside the main idea of the text.

_____ Grace and her brothers traveled far to see their mother.

_____ Grace and her brothers felt disappointed that their mother didn't accept them.

_____ Geneva did not appear the way Grace imagined her to be.

The <u>four</u> statements below "support" the main idea. Fill in the blanks with the correct word.

(a) Grace felt _____ if the woman they were visiting was actually her mother.

(b) When Geneva did not believe they were her children, Grace told her that she had brought her _____.

(c) Grace and her brothers pleading with Geneva to accept them seemed _____.

(d) Ashley reminded them that Geneva had a mental _____ and may need time to accept them.

Sequencing
Circle the letter for the correct answer based on the events in Chapter 2.

1. What did Grace think when she first looked at Geneva?
    a. She decided that she wasn't her mother right away.
    b. It triggered memories of how she desired to take care of her.
    c. She did not doubt that the woman was her mother because she felt excited.

2. Did Geneva look anything like how Grace expected her to be?
    a. No. Grace was surprised that Geneva did not look like her and was not tall.
    b. Yes. Geneva looked like her youthful self in the pictures, but aged now.
    c. No. Geneva did not look like she would be related to them at all.

3. Did Geneva accept the gift that Grace had brought for her?
    a. Although tempted to accept it at first, she refused it.
    b. Yes, she was very interested in the gift and accepted it.
    c. No, she refused it before Grace even took it out of her bag.

Themes: Expectation Vs. Reality

The theme is the main idea or underlying message in a literary work, which may be stated directly or indirectly. One of the themes in this chapter is "expectation vs. reality".

Grace has certain expectations about the time she would meet her mother. However, the outcome of the event turned out to be different.

Complete the table below based on what Grace expected to happen versus what actually happened when she met her mother.

Expectations	Reality

Literary Techniques: Emotive Language

Emotive language is a literary device that writers employ in order to stir the reader's emotions. They may intentionally use certain emotional words to kindle feelings of empathy, sadness or joy in the reader.

Pick 3 words from Chapter 2 that the writer has used for the following:

Sadness: _____   _____   _____

Identifying Cause and Effect

"The way Geneva looked each of us in the face and rejected us without any remorse. I absolutely did not like the woman who we had just encountered, and I did not want her as my mother."

What is the Cause? _____
_____

What is the Effect? _____
_____

Textual Evidence

Cite *two* examples from the text to show that Geneva was uncomfortable and suspicious about her visitors.

Textual Evidence	Textual Evidence
1.	2.

Character Trait Discussion

The character trait for Chapter 1 is "sedulous".
Sedulous means careful and using a lot of effort.

Read the statement below. Then choose one of the questions below and answer it. Write your answer in the space provided then discuss it with your group.

In this chapter, we see how sedulous Grace is about visiting Geneva, despite the risk of meeting the wrong woman. She has always put in a lot of effort for this cause and finally accomplished it.

1. Would you remain sedulous even if what you are trying to achieve will take years to accomplish? Why or why not?

2. Describe something that you would work sedulously for and state your reasons.

3. Do you know someone who is sedulous about something? Describe them and their cause.

Lesson Three - Worksheet

This lesson coincides with Chapter 3 of the book, 'Reuniting with Mother'. The purpose of this lesson is to analyze clues and key information in the text to interpret the outcome of the main event. **Chapter Three – "Will Mother Accept Us?"**

Main Idea and Supporting Details
Place an X on the line beside the main idea of the text.

_____ Grace was determined to get Geneva to warm up to her and her brothers.

_____ Grace coaxed Geneva into talking by buying some of her favorite things.

_____ Geneva honestly did not recognize Grace and her brothers.

The *four* statements below "support" the main idea. Fill in the blanks with the correct word.

(a) Miss Davis told Grace that if she brought Geneva _____, she would sit with her and talk.

(b) Geneva got off the bus and _____ across the street towards the boarding home.

(c) Grace handed Geneva a list of _____ that Jerome had made for her.

(d) She also gave Geneva a copy of her own _____.

Sequencing
Look at the following events from Chapter 3 and number the boxes according to the order in which they happened.

After the blue bus arrived, Geneva got off and started walking to the boarding house.	Miss Davis directed Grace to the corner store where she could buy the things for Geneva.

Once inside Geneva's room, Grace handed her the items she had bought, list of contact details that Jerome made and showed her some pictures of her family.

Grace and her brothers waited anxiously for the blue bus to arrive with Geneva.	Grace and her brother bought cigarettes, coffee, shampoo, lotion, deodorant and a bar of soap for Geneva.

Literary Techniques: Descriptive Language

Through descriptive language, the author informs readers about what a person, place, object or situation is like.

How does Grace describe Geneva's room in chapter 3?

Furniture: _____

Decoration: _____

Colors: _____

Tidiness: _____

Literary Elements: Mood

Moods in literature not only describe how a person feels, but also the atmosphere of groups of people, places, time periods, events, etc.

Based on your analysis of Chapter 3, how is the mood at the beginning of the chapter and at the end?

Beginning	End

Identifying Cause and Effect

"I felt amazed because this was the first sign of her showing that she actually knew who we were! This made me feel a little more confident that this woman was indeed my mother."

What is the Cause? _____

What is the Effect? _____

Textual Evidence

Cite two examples from the text to show that Geneva cared for Grace and her siblings.

Textual Evidence	Explanation
1.	1.
2.	2.

Character Trait Discussion
The character trait for Chapter 3 is "open-minded".
Open-minded means you are willing to consider new ideas without prejudice.

Read the statement below. Then choose one of the questions below and answer it. Write your answer in the space provided then discuss it with your group.

Grace has been open-minded ever since she began the journey of searching for her mother. She has tried different approaches, accepted suggestions from other people and even bought things for Geneva as suggested by Miss Davis.

1. Do you consider yourself an open-minded individual? Explain why or why not with examples.

2. Name one advantages and one disadvantages of being open-minded?

3. How is having an open mind important when it comes to achieving your goals?

Lesson Four - Worksheet

This lesson coincides with Chapter 4 of the book, 'Reuniting with Mother'. The purpose of this lesson is to observe and analyze character transformation.
Chapter Four – "Reunited"

Main Idea and Supporting Details

Place an X on the line beside the main idea of the text.

_____ Geneva was not comfortable with meeting Grace's brothers together.

_____ Geneva finally opened up and started talking about some personal things.

_____ Geneva wanted to know where her other children were as well.

The <u>four</u> statements below "support" the main idea. Fill in the blanks with the correct word.

(a) Geneva told Grace and Terrence that she had _____ more children after she left.

(b) Geneva and Calvin were together for _____ years.

(c) Geneva confirmed that she did not give Grace her middle name, which was _____.

(d) Geneva's favorite food was _____.

Sequencing

Number the events of Chapter 4 in the order they happened.

( )   After that, she asked to see Terrence and opened up while he was there.

( )   The brothers were confused as to why she wanted to see Grayson first.

( )   She divulged some personal information during that time.

( )   Geneva agreed to see Grace's brothers one at a time.

( )   Grace and Terrence decide to come back the next day to have dinner with Geneva.

( )   Next, Geneva asked to see "Devon" since that's how she remembered him.

Plot Analysis: Falling Action

The falling action happens right after the climax in a story, when the main problem starts to resolve. This is where the tension arising from the story's main conflict starts to decrease. The falling action is also referred to as "Denouement".

In Chapter 4, we have started to see a change in Geneva's attitude towards Grace and her brothers. Compile information from Chapters 1 to 4, and write a brief note on what the climax and falling action is for this story.

Reuniting with Mother	
Climax	**Falling Action**

Identifying Cause and Effect

"This was an amazing moment for me, because I had longed to find the siblings my mother had after she left."

What is the Cause? _____

What is the Effect? _____

Character Transformation

Using the information from Chapters 1-4, write your observations on how Geneva behaved with Grace and her brothers at the beginning, and how she starts to change in Chapter 4.

Geneva	
Before	**After**

Character Trait Discussion

The character trait for Chapter 4 is "patient".

Patient means you are able to accept or tolerate delays without getting annoyed easily.

Read the statement below. Then choose <u>one</u> of the questions below and answer it. Write your answer in the space provided then discuss it with your group.

Grace had been tremendously patient with her mother until she agreed to see her brothers one by one.

1. Would you be patient if you were in Grace's situation? Why or why not?

2. Who is the most patient person you know and why?

3. Is it better to be patient and understanding, or be demanding for faster results? Please explain why.

_____

_____

_____

_____

_____

Lesson Five - Worksheet

This lesson coincides with Chapter 5 of the book, 'Reuniting with Mother'. The purpose of this lesson is to study the resolution of the story and interpret the author's intent.
Chapter Five – "Our Final Visit With Mother"

Main Idea and Supporting Details
Place an X on the line beside the main idea of the text.

_____ Grace and her brothers had a chicken dinner with Geneva on the final visit.

_____ Grace wanted to know why Geneva left her and her brothers.

_____ Grace wishes that Geneva would accept their offers and move to Kansas City.

The <u>four</u> statements below "support" the main idea. Fill in the blanks with the correct word.

(a) Geneva told Grace that she had some _____ to take care of before she could move.

(b) Terrence told Geneva that if she moved to Kansas City, they could have her _____ fixed and take her to all of her _____.

(c) Grace was shocked that Geneva preferred to live in the _____ place she was living.

(d) Geneva had lived in the boarding home for _____ years.

Plot Analysis: Resolution
The resolution in a story happens after the falling action and it typically where the story ends. In the resolution, all the conflicts are resolved and the characters come to an agreement. However, the ending of the story need not always be a happy one. Sometimes authors will end stories in such a way that there are future possibilities for a continuation.

Answer each question briefly to uncover the resolution of this story in Chapter 5.

(a) What agreement did the characters come to at the end of the chapter?

(b) Was the ending of "Reuniting with Mother" a happy or sad one? Explain.

(c) Do you think there is a possibility for the story to continue in the future? Give reasons.

Identifying Cause and Effect

"We all realized that our hands were somewhat tied since that final decision would have to be hers."

What is the Cause? _____

What is the Effect? _____

Textual Evidence

Cite one example from the text to show that the boarding home was not a good place for Geneva to live happily.

Textual Evidence	Explanation

Author's Intention

Authors write stories for a variety of reasons. They may want to write the story to get a theme across or even just to teach a moral. It is important to understand the author's purpose for writing the story in order to better understand the text.

Complete the table below to decode the author's intention for writing "Finding Mother After Five Decades" and "Reuniting with Mother".

Name of the Author	**Grace LaJoy Henderson**
Name(s) of the Book(s)	
Themes in the Story	
Main Character's Name	
Main Character's Traits	
Main Character's Conflict	
Did the main character resolve the conflict in the end?	

Based on the information you wrote in the table above, write a brief note on what you think the author wants you to take from this story.

Story Summary

Fill in the boxes below to create a brief summary for "Reuniting with Mother After Five Decades".

What happens at the beginning? Introduce the characters and what they are doing.

What is the main conflict of the story?

What is the main idea of the story?

How were the characters able to resolve the conflict?

What happens at the end of the story?

Character Trait Discussion

The character trait for Chapter 3 is "tenaciousness".
Tenaciousness refers to someone or something that holds on firmly.

Read the statement below. Then choose one of the questions below and answer it. Write your answer in the space provided then discuss it with your group.

Grace's tenaciousness helped her to find her mother although it took forty-nine years.

1. When some goals take longer to achieve, it becomes easier to give up. What would motivate you to be tenacious in this case?

2. Name someone you know who is tenacious? Explain why you think they are tenacious.

3. Are there disadvantages to be being tenacious? If so, what are they?

_____
_____
_____
_____
_____
_____
_____
_____
_____
_____
_____
_____

Book 3

After the Reunion

Answer Keys
Chapters 1-12

Lesson One - Worksheet

This lesson coincides with Chapter One of the book, "After the Reunion: A Story of Acceptance". The purpose of this lesson is to analyze and evaluate the author's emotions post reuniting with her mother. **Chapter One – "Returning Home After the Reunion"**

Main Idea and Supporting Details

Place an "X" on the line beside the "main idea" of the story.

_____ **Grace felt disturbed and unhappy about finding her mother in deprived conditions.**

_____ Grace was expecting to find her mother in a safe environment.

_____ Grace's mother, Geneva was living in a building with beggars and peddlers.

The <u>four</u> statements below "support" the main idea. Fill in the blanks with the correct word.

(a) Grace took a few days off work after the _____ because she was not feeling well.

(b) Grace was _____ with the way her mother was living.

(c) She felt so _____ that she needed someone trustworthy to talk to.

(d) Grace was in shock because she had found her mother living in _____.

Sequencing

The following sentences tell what happens in the story. Read them and number them in the correct order.

(a) Grace emailed Elsie about her reunion with her mother.   ( )

(b) Grace felt her mother should not be living a deprived life.   ( )

(c) The woman on the counseling hotline consoled Grace.   ( )

(d) Grace appreciated the woman's interest in her story.   ( )

(e) Grace contacted Elsie for information about her sibling's adoption.   ( )

(f) Grace felt downhearted and needed someone to talk to.   ( )

(g) Grace did not feel well because of her mother's poor living condition.   ( )

(h) Grace found a number for a counseling hotline.   ( )

(i) Grace told the woman she had often thought of starting a homeless shelter.   ( )

(j) Grace felt hopeful as she waited for a response from Elsie.   ( )

Plot Analysis

Now That you have put the sentences above in the correct order, write which is the beginning, the climax and the end.

The Beginning:

The Climax:

The End:

Point of View

Point of view is the voice or persona that the author creates in order to tell the story.
Which point of view does the author use in this story?

(a) first person   (b) third-person limited   (c) omniscient   (d) objective

Check the line beside the word that describe what type of selection this is:

_____ Fiction

_____ Non-fiction

Identifying Cause and Effect

"With that burden lifted, I felt happy for the rest of the day and was able to return to work the next day feeling refreshed."

What is the Cause? _____

What is the Effect? _____

Comparing and Contrasting

Compare Grace's feelings before and after having the counseling session.

Her feelings before the session	Her feelings after the session

Character Analysis

Analyze the main character and describe her with a trait. Support your choice with relevant evidences and examples.

Character Name: *Grace / the protagonist / the main character / the author*

The character is:	*Because*
Example: helpful	She wanted to start a homeless shelter.

Contextual Meaning

Read the following excerpt from the story with the highlighted word. Circle True or False below.

"After a **meticulous** online search, I found the number of a counseling hotline where I could speak with someone freely without revealing my true identity."

The word "meticulous" means careful.   **True / False**

Character Trait Discussion

The Character Trait for Lesson One is "benevolent".
Benevolent means well-meaning and kindly.

Read the statement below. Then choose one of the questions below and answer it. Write your answer in the space provided then discuss it with your group.

Grace is benevolent towards her mother and wants to make her life more comfortable. She feels bad about her mother's deprived living conditions and wants to find her a better place to stay.

1. Are you a benevolent person? What are some acts of kindness that you have done?
2. Mention someone you know that is benevolent. State your reasons.
3. Would you do caring things for a loved one, even if they cannot do things for you? Why or why not?

_____

_____

_____

_____

_____

_____

_____

_____

_____

_____

_____

Lesson Two - Worksheet

This lesson coincides with Chapter Two of the book, "After the Reunion: A Story of Acceptance". The purpose of this lesson is to understand the setting and the level of care that the author has for her mother.
Chapter Two – "My Search for a Place for Mother"

Main Idea and Supporting Details
Place an "X" on the line beside the "main idea" of the story.

_____ Grace was ready to remove her mother from the boarding home.

_____ Grace had always dreamed of finding her mother and taking care of her.

_____ Grace did not expect to find her mother living in such poor conditions.

The <u>four</u> statements below "support" the main idea. Fill in the blanks with the correct word.

(a) Grace began to think about _____ her mother from where she was to Kansas City.

(b) _____ warned Grace and her siblings that they were not going to happy when they see her living conditions.

(c) Grace _____ that her mother would be more than ready to let them care for her.

(d) Grace began discussing with the boarding home office manager about the type of

_____ that she should be looking for in Kansas City.1

Sequencing
Number the following lines from Chapter 2 to put them in the correct order.

_____ Grace had been warned that she wouldn't be happy seeing her mother's living condition.

_____ She asked for the packet of information to share with her brothers and mother.

_____ Ever since she was a little girl, Grace had dreamed of finding her mother.

_____ Grace chose the second assisted living center.

_____ Grace discussed with April about the required facility for her mother in Kansas City.

_____ April provided all the required information to search for an assisted living center for her mother.

Point of View

What is the point of view in Chapter 2? Circle the letter for the correct answer.

(a) first-person   (b) second-person   (c) third-person

Explain your reason here:

Answer: *The narrator is using the pronouns "I" and "me" when narrating the story. This shows that she is telling the story from her point of view. Therefore, it is the first-person point of view.*

Genre

Check the line beside the term that best describes this chapter.

_____ Personal Narrative

_____ Science Fiction

Author's Purpose

What do you think the author's purpose for this chapter is?

Circle the letter for the correct answer.

(a) To entertain with a story about a woman's search for a place for her mother.
(b) To persuade the reader about looking for safe places for old people.
(c) To inform about an assisted living facility.

Identifying Cause and Effect

"In my search for an assisted living facility for her, a nurse told me that since she has a serious mental illness, she would also be eligible to live in a nursing home."

What is the Cause? _____

What is the Effect? _____

Comparing and Contrasting

Compare and contrast the first and second assisted living facility and fill the graphic organizer.

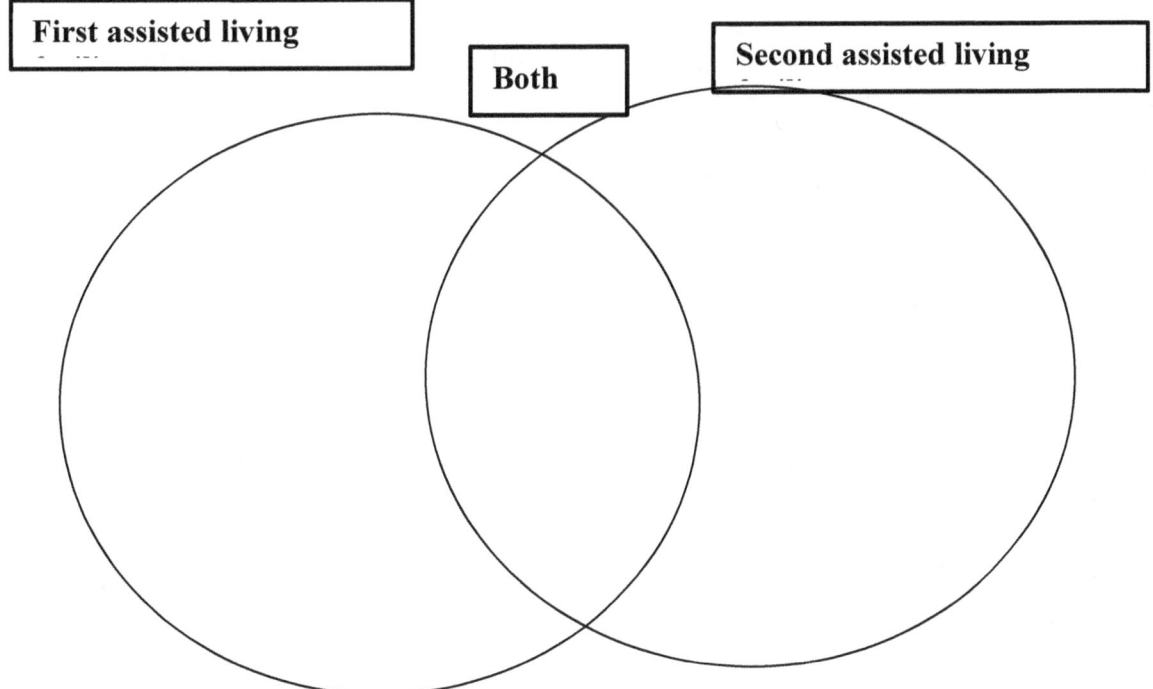

Interpreting and Evaluating Information

After visiting both places, what made Grace like the second one the best?

Character Trait Evidence

List five character traits of Geneva, Grace's mother.

(1) _____

(2) _____

(3) _____

(4) _____

(5) _____

Contextual Meaning

Read the following line from Chapter 2 with the highlighted word and circle the best meaning for it.

"After the reunion, I continued reviewing the benefits and **amenities** of numerous facilities." What does the word "amenities" mean?"

(a) features   (b) convenience   (c) both a & b

Character Trait Discussion

The Character Trait for Lesson Two is "thoughtful".
Thoughtful means showing consideration for the needs of other people.

Read the statement below. Then choose one of the questions below and answer it. Write your answer in the space provided then discuss it with your group.

Grace is very thoughtful in finding a comfortable place for her mother to stay. This shows that she is a very caring person.

1. What would you do if you found a long lost relative living in poor conditions?

2. Do you think it is important to look after elderly people? Why or why not?

3. Think about a person you know who is thoughtful? What types of thoughtful things have they done?

_____

_____

_____

_____

_____

_____

_____

_____

Lesson Three - Worksheet

This lesson coincides with Chapter Three of the book, "After the Reunion: A Story of Acceptance". The purpose of this lesson is to understand the kind of relationship the author has with her mother post reunion through their conversations.
Chapter Three – "A Typical Phone Call With Mother"

Main Idea and Supporting Details
Place an "X" on the line beside the "main idea" of the story.

_____ Geneva made up excuses whenever she wanted to get off the phone.

_____ Grace learned some fun things about her mother when they talked.

_____ Grace's phone calls with her mother became more frequent as time passed.

The four statements below "support" the main idea. Fill in the blanks with the correct word.

(a) Grace and her mother would initially only talk _____ a month.

(b) After a short while, they would be on the phone every other _____.

(c) In a later phone conversation, Geneva reminded Grace of her _____ and _____.

(d) Grace felt happy that her mother was able to _____ exactly what was important to her.

Sequencing
Read the following extract from Chapter 3 and answer the questions that follow.

"It seemed she was asking me those questions for a few reasons. The first, she may have appreciated me calling her and she enjoyed talking to me. The second, she could have wanted me to feel like she really wanted to talk to me, especially since a lot of the time she would prefer to be in her bed resting her hip. A third, she might have been aiming towards being kind to her daughter whom she knew loved her."

Which words from this extract show sequence?

Author's Purpose
Which question could best help someone figure out that the author's purpose in this chapter is to entertain?

a) Did the author give me new information?
b) Did the author teach me how to make something?
c) Did the author ask me to do anything?
d) Did the author tell me a story about her relationship with her mother?

Identifying Cause and Effect
"Then after a few more words back and forth, she said, "Well, I want to go lay in my bed and rest a little.""

What is the Cause? _____

What is the Effect? _____

Interpreting and Evaluating Information
Evaluate the mother-daughter relationship in this chapter by analyzing communication.

Contextual Meaning
Read the following line from Chapter 2 with the highlighted word and choose the best meaning for it.

"A huge smile would break up on my face before regaining my **composure** enough to say, "Hello, Mother, how are you doing?""

(a) instability   (b) excitement   (c) self-control

Character Analysis
Cross out the adjective(s), which are not suitable to describe Grace.

Sensitive	Kind-hearted	excited
Concerned	carefree	dutiful
Emotional	Caring	forgetful

Character Trait Discussion
The Character Trait for Lesson Three is "altruistic".
Altruistic means showing a disinterested and selfless concern for the well-being of others.

Read the statement below. Then choose one of the questions below and answer it. Write your answer in the space provided then discuss it with your group.

Grace is altruistic about her mother's needs and phoning to check on her as often as possible.

1. Describe how you communicate with your parent(s). What are some things you do for your parent(s) without being?

2. Do you think it is important to check on family members who are far away? Why or why not?

3. What are some benefits of showing concern for others?

_____
_____
_____
_____
_____
_____
_____

Lesson Four - Worksheet

This lesson coincides with Chapter Four of the book, "After the Reunion: A Story of Acceptance". The purpose of this lesson is to understand the importance of the author's journey for the second time and to analyze the bond she has with her own daughter.
Chapter Four – "My Second Trip to Visit Mother"

Main Idea and Supporting Details

Place an "X" on the line beside the "main idea" of the story.

_____ Grace decided to take her daughter, Arica with her on the trip.

_____ Grace decided to visit her mother a second time to find out why she left.

_____ Jerome was concerned about Grace and Arica driving to Geneva's state.

The <u>four</u> statements below "support" the main idea. Fill in the blanks with the correct word.

(a) Leading up the second trip, Geneva acting very _____ about Grace coming to visit.

(b) Grace could not wait for her mother to meet _____.

(c) Grace felt extremely _____ even through Geneva would probably not agree to move.

(d) Grace and her daughter pulled out many _____ that she thought Geneva would appreciate.

Sequencing

Read the following lines from Chapter 4 and put them in the correct order.

(a) They both laughed listened to music.   ( )

(b) Grace was planning to share some information with her mother about assisted living facilities.   ( )

(c) Geneva was very excited about their visit and asked repeatedly about the date of their arrival.   ( )

(d) Grace planned a trip to visit her mother along with her daughter, Arica.   ( )

(e) Grace and her daughter decided to drive a rental car.   ( )

(f) While preparing for the trip, Grace packed some albums.   ( )

(g) Grace was excited and happy at the same time for her mother to meet Arica. ( )

(h) Grace was honored and joyful to receive her daughter's avocado bread. That had always been one of her favorite finger foods. ( )

(i) Terrance pitched in some cash to help them pay for the trip. ( )

(j) They left the evening before June 8. ( )

Author's Purpose
An author writes for one of three reasons:
to entertain, to inform (teach) or to persuade (convince)

Circle the author's purpose in this chapter?

(a) to entertain

(b) to inform

(c) to persuade

Explain the reason for your answer:

Identifying Cause and Effect

"During our reunion visit, I noted that the more she looked at the pictures, the more it began to "click" for her that we were her children. The more she realized we were her children, the more she opened up, and eventually accepted us."

What is the Cause? _____

What is the Effect? _____

Interpreting and Evaluating Information
What was the purpose of Grace's second visit to her mother?

Comparing and Contrasting

Compare Grace with her daughter Arica and state the similarities between them.

Grace	Similarities	Arica

Language: Idioms

An idiom is a common expression understood figuratively, as the literal meaning makes no sense. Many idioms have been used in this chapter. Write three idioms from Chapter 4.

(a) _____

(b) _____

(c) _____

Inference

Read the short extract from Chapter 4, and place an "X" on the statements that are valid inferences for this extract.

"As I was biting into the delicious snack that my daughter had so carefully prepared, I thought about how grateful I felt that finding my mother had resulted in my sharing this special moment together with my daughter."

_____ While traveling to visit her mother, Grace and her daughter were having special moments together.

_____ Traveling to visit her mother ultimately resulted in Grace and her daughter getting time to bond.

_____ Grace was excited for her daughter to meet her grandmother.

_____ Grace and her daughter did not sleep in a motel like Jerome suggested.

Character Analysis
Circle all of the traits that suitable for Grace's brothers: Jerome and Terrence.

Devastated   Helping   Concerned   Supportive   Guilt   Insecure   Excited   Caring

Character Trait Discussion
The Character Trait for Lesson Four is "loving".
Loving means feeling and showing love or great care.

Read the statement below. Then choose <u>one</u> of the questions below and answer it. Write your answer in the space provided then discuss it with your group.

Grace is loving in the sense that she wants to do everything she can for her mother's well-being and even bring her back home. We can see the same trait in her daughter Arica as well.

1. Describe your relationship with your mother and all things you do together.

2. Why do you think it is important to spend time with your family?

3. If you were in Grace's position, would you drive all the way to visit your mother? Why or why not?

___

___

___

___

___

___

___

___

___

Lesson Five - Worksheet

This lesson coincides with Chapter Five of the book, "After the Reunion: A Story of Acceptance". The purpose of this lesson is to analyze the author's feelings during the second visit to her mother.
Chapter Five – "Arriving on Thursday Evening"

Main Idea and Supporting Details
Place an "X" on the line beside the "main idea" of the story.

_____ Grace was excited about seeing her mother right away when they arrived.

_____ Grace was happy and proud to finally introduce Arica to her mother.

_____ The photos that Grace brought on the trip captured her mother's attention.

The <u>four</u> statements below "support" the main idea. Fill in the blanks with the correct word.

(a) The _____ of driving to the boarding home where she lived was intense.

(b) Grace was concerned about returning to that _____ and _____ neighborhood.

(c) Grace felt that her mother was worth any _____ that she would experience to see her.

(d) Geneva did not know the exact _____ that Grace and Arica were coming.

Sequencing
Write briefly in each box what happens in Chapter 5.

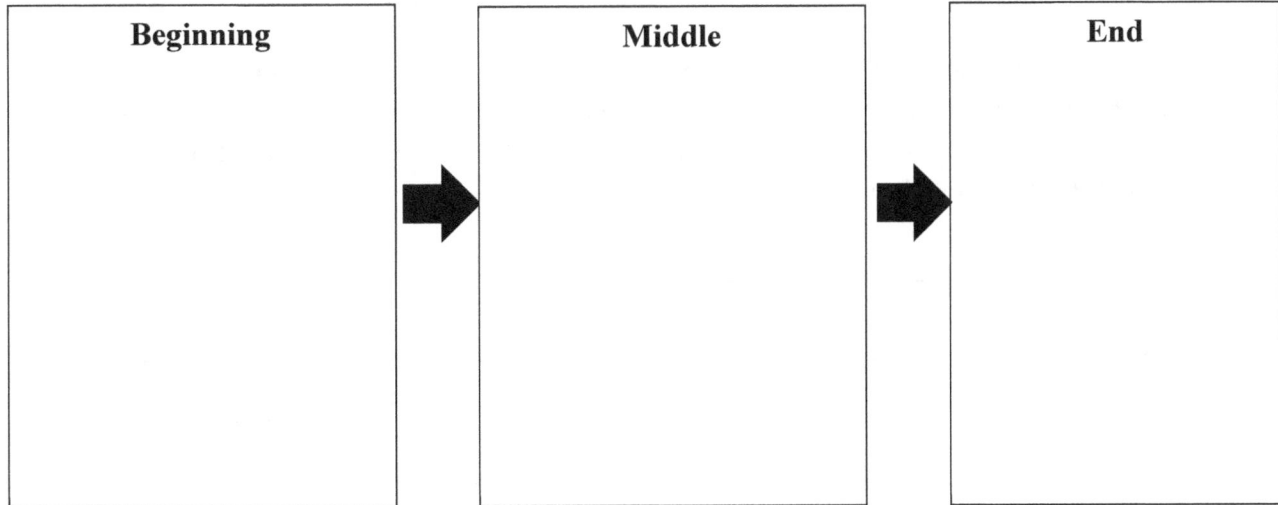

Point of View

The passage below is in first person point of view. Rewrite it in the third person point of view.
"It was around five o'clock in the evening of June 7th when we left Kansas City; and it was around five o'clock in the evening of June 8th when we arrived at our out-of-town hotel. Arica and I were both tired and felt like resting, but I was too excited and wanted to go see my mother right away."

Author's Purpose

The author's purpose of this selection is to entertain because the author holds readers' attention with enjoyment.

(a) True   (b) False

Identifying Cause and Effect

"She said they had done many nice things to the house, like fixing major holes in the walls and painting. She explained that she was used to being there. Furthermore, she expressed that she did not want to leave at this time. Although I was saddened, I understood how she felt, and most of all, I truly appreciated her honesty."

What is the Cause? _____

What is the Effect? _____

Literary Techniques: Descriptive Language
Write the author's descriptions for the boarding home in the boxes below.

Scenery and View	Scents and Smells
Sounds and Noises	**Sensation and Surface**

Character Analysis
Grace was having a mixture of feelings at different parts of the story.
Analyze Grace's emotions before and after meeting her mother again.

Before	After

Character Trait Discussion
The Character Trait for Lesson Five is "accommodating".
Accommodating means willing to fit someone's wishes or needs.

Read the statement below. Then choose one of the questions below and answer it. Write your answer in the space provided then discuss it with your group.
Grace is very accommodating towards her mother. She does not pressure her into moving to Kansas City even though she would like her to. Yet, she continues to care for her mother.

1. What would you do to convince your mother to move closer to you?

2. Do you think it is better to respect someone's wishes to stay where they are, or compel them to move because the place is bad? Explain your answer.

3. Think of an accommodating person who you know and explain why you feel that person is accommodating.

___

Lesson Six

This lesson coincides with Chapter Six of the book, "After the Reunion: A Story of Acceptance". The purpose of this lesson is to analyze the author's mother and her connection with the people around her.
Chapter Six – "Day Two of Our Visit - Friday"

Main Idea and Supporting Details
Place an "X" on the line beside the "main idea" of the story.

_____ Donna was shocked to know that Grace and Arica were Geneva's family.

_____ Grace thought about the fun they would have participating in activities with Geneva.

_____ All the workers thought that Geneva was nice, quiet and didn't bother anyone.

The <u>four</u> statements below "support" the main idea. Fill in the blanks with the correct word.

(a) Geneva told Grace and Arica to come to the _____ around noon.

(b) When they arrived at the address, they met the center manager, _____.

(c) Donna gave Grace her _____ and welcomed her to call anytime.

(d) Grace felt _____ for expecting to participate in activities with Geneva at the center.

Character Analysis: Geneva
Analyze Geneva's character by giving her two traits based on this chapter. Support your choice by citing relevant examples from the text.

Traits	Example from the Text

Identifying Cause and Effect

"She mentioned they recently had some difficulty getting her to take it consistently. She told me a story of how the workers noticed she had been acting angry and cussing at people more than usual. The staff came up with a bright idea to check under the mattress on her bed. There they found the pills she was supposed to be taking daily, but she had been hiding them instead. Donna said she had to remind my mother that if she did not take her medication that she could end up locked up in a mental hospital again. Having a fear of going back there, she started taking it regularly."

What is the Cause? _____

What is the Effect? _____

-or-

What is the Cause? _____

What is the Effect? _____

Interpreting and Evaluating Information
What are the things that Donna liked about Geneva?

Contextual Meaning
Read the following line from Chapter 6 with the highlighted word and choose the best meaning for it.

"I woke up the next morning, **envisioning** the fun we would have sitting in the center, participating in activities with my mother."

(a) disregarding　　　　　　(b) neglecting　　　　　　(c) visualizing

Character Trait Discussion

The Character Trait for Lesson Six is "acquiescent".

Acquiescent means ready to accept something without protest, or to do what someone else wants.

Read the statement below. Then choose one of the questions below and answer it. Write your answer in the space provided then discuss it with your group.

Grace is acquiescent in regard to her mother's needs. She arrives at the center hoping to participate in activities with her mother.

1. Would you be willing to participate in activities with an elderly person?

    Explain why or why not.

2. Have you ever been acquiescent just to please someone? Describe the situation.

3. Do you think it good to be acquiescent all the time? Discuss you answer.

_____

_____

_____

_____

_____

_____

_____

_____

_____

_____

_____

_____

Lesson Seven - Worksheet

This lesson coincides with Chapter Seven of the book, "After the Reunion: A Story of Acceptance". The purpose of this lesson is to analyze the author's mother and her connection with the people around her.
Chapter Seven – "Day Two of Our Visit – Talking with Mother"

Main Idea and Supporting Details
Place an "X" on the line beside the "main idea" of the story.

_____ Geneva talks about her husband and the birth order of all her children.

_____ Geneva is concerned about Carla missing.

_____ Grace was surprised to hear that her father had been traveling even before Geneva left.

The <u>four</u> statements below "support" the main idea. Fill in the blanks with the correct word.

(a) Geneva and Grace's father moved to another state and lived there for _____ years.

(b) Geneva told Arica that her husband was _____ and _____ to her.

(c) Geneva remembered buying a _____ for Carla.

(d) Geneva did not remember buying Grace chocolate covered _____.

Literary Devices: Flashback
Flashbacks are interruptions that writers do to insert past events, in order to provide background or context to the current events of a narrative.
Cite two examples of flashbacks from this chapter.

Example 1:	Example 2:

Literary Elements: Tone
The tone is the feeling or the atmosphere set by the author. What is author's tone in this chapter? Circle the letter for the correct answer.

(a) gloomy   (b) ironic   (c) nostalgic

Identifying Cause and Effect

"Right. It's a nice place to live for now. You never know what's going to happen when you look ahead, you know. Right now, you know, I'd rather stay here, you know."

What is the Cause? _____

What is the Effect? _____

Interpreting and Evaluating Information
Write two reasons why Grace's father left her and his siblings alone at home.

Reason 1:

Reason 2:

Contextual Meaning
Read the following line from Chapter 7 with the highlighted word and circle the best meaning for it.

"I found that **intriguing**. I asked her if she remembered walking me to a convenience store in Kansas City."

(a) fascinating   (b) uninteresting   (c) boring

Inference
What can you infer from the following lines?

"Right. It's a nice place to live for now. You never know what's going to happen when you look ahead, you know. Right now, you know, I'd rather stay here, you know."

Character Trait Discussion

The Character Trait for Lesson Seven is "affable".
Affable means friendly, good-natured and easy to talk to.

*Read the statement below. Then choose one of the questions below and answer it.
Write your answer in the space provided then discuss it with your group.*

Geneva was affable with Grace and Arica during their time together. She did not make them feel unwelcome or uncomfortable during their conversation.

1. Are you an affable person? Explain why or why not.

2. Mention someone you can talk about anything with. State at least one reason.

3. What are two benefits of being an affable person?

_____

_____

_____

_____

_____

_____

_____

_____

_____

_____

_____

_____

Lesson Eight - Worksheet

This lesson coincides with Chapter Eight of the book, "After the Reunion: A Story of Acceptance". The purpose of this lesson is to study some background information in order to understand the author's mother better.
Chapter Eight – "Day Two of Our Visit – Talking About Moving"

Main Idea and Supporting Details
Place an "X" on the line beside the "main idea" of the story.

_____ Geneva told Grace and Arica some stories of her childhood.

_____ Grace showed Geneva the information on the facility she had picked for her.

_____ Grace was not ready to take long-distance responsibility for her mother.

The <u>four</u> statements below "support" the main idea. Fill in the blanks with the correct word.

(a) _____ had insisted that Grace show Geneva the information about the facility.

(b) Grace pulled out a _____ which contained all the information.

(c) Grace told Geneva that she can leave her _____ in her own room at the facility because they would be safe.

(d) Geneva stated that the facility looked like _____ and that she was not ready for anything like that.

Character Analysis
What can you tell about the Geneva's character based on the childhood stories she told Arica?

Geneva's Childhood	
Who were her family?	
What were some activities she indulged in?	
Was she an obedient or mischievous child? Explain why.	

Identifying Cause and Effect

"I felt surprised, yet grateful when Arica asked the question about how Mother felt when she met us."

What is the Cause? <u>when Arica asked the question about how Mother felt when she met us.</u>

What is the Effect? <u>I felt surprised, yet grateful</u>

Interpreting and Evaluating Information
Mention three ways in which Grace tried to convince her mother to move to Kansas City.

Comparing and Contrasting
Compare Geneva's condition with and without her medication.

With Medication	Without Medication

Character Trait Discussion
The Character Trait for Lesson Eight is "enthusiastic".
Enthusiastic means showing intense interest and excitement.

Read the statement below. Then choose one of the questions below and answer it. Write your answer in the space provided then discuss it with your group.

At the beginning of the chapter, Grace is enthusiastic about sharing the information about the facility she picked for her mother. She hopes that her mother would be convinced to move.

1. Name one thing that you have been enthusiastic about sharing with your family?

2. Name 3 things you are enthusiastic about?

3. Do you think it is important to be enthusiastic? Why or why not?

_____

_____

_____

_____

_____

_____

_____

_____

_____

_____

_____

_____

Lesson Nine - Worksheet

This lesson coincides with Chapter Nine of the book, "After the Reunion: A Story of Acceptance". The purpose of this lesson is to observe some similarities the author has with her mother.
Chapter Nine – "Day Three of Our Visit - Saturday"

Main Idea and Supporting Details
Place an "X" on the line beside the "main idea" of the story.

_____ Geneva bought some soda pop for Grace and Arica.

_____ Grace had forgotten to make the video call with Terrence and Grayson.

_____ Grace was able to observe her mother and understand where she got certain traits and features from.

The <u>four</u> statements below "support" the main idea. Fill in the blanks with the correct word.

(a) Grace noticed her mother walking on her _____.

(b) Grace also noticed that her _____ was similar to her mother's.

(c) Grace and her mother laughed at each other's _____.

(d) Realizing where she got some of her _____ and _____

from made Grace appreciate herself more.

Summarizing
Summarize the following paragraph in two sentences.

"After a while, Mother finally entered the living room with a big smile on her face. Her backpack was in one hand, and two bottles of soda pop was in the other. She held the necks of the bottles in between her fingers. The proud look on her face indicated that she was confident we would be happy about getting the drinks; and that we would feel it was worth the wait to quench our thirst at last."

Identifying Cause and Effect

"After that, I made a regular voice call to Terrance and found out he had already left Grayson's house. They had waited for my call for an hour, then gave up. I told him how sorry I was and that if he went back around to Grayson's house, I would call again. He assured me it was okay and said he did not have time to go back over."

What is the Cause? _____

What is the Effect? _____

Comparing and Contrasting
Compare Geneva and Grace by stating three similarities between them.

Geneva	Similarities	Grace
	• • •	

Interpreting and Evaluating Information
Explain what Geneva meant when she said that she would feel embarrassed about "hopping" into the restaurant.

Character Trait Analysis: Geneva

In this chapter, we learn more about Geneva's character and personality. Describe Geneva's character by stating some traits for her and supporting them with evidences.

Traits	Examples

Character Trait Discussion

The Character Trait for Lesson Nine is "appreciation".
Appreciation means recognition and enjoyment of the good qualities of someone or something.

Read the statement below. Then choose <u>one</u> of the questions below and answer it. Write your answer in the space provided then discuss it with your group.
Grace appreciated herself more after noticing some similarities between herself and her mother.

1. Describe three things that you appreciate about yourself and explain why.

2. Who do you appreciate the most in your life and why?

3. Do you feel it is better to appreciate the things we have and not complain? Why or why not?

_____

_____

_____

Lesson Ten - Worksheet

This lesson coincides with Chapter Ten of the book, "After the Reunion: A Story of Acceptance". The purpose of this lesson is to observe the author's feelings and reaction to an unexpected turn or events.
Ten – "Day Four of Our Visit - Sunday"

Main Idea and Supporting Details
Place an "X" on the line beside the "main idea" of the story.

_____ Grace bought Geneva some new and comfortable sandals.
_____ Grace felt disappointed that Geneva refused to go out to dinner.
_____ Everyone at the boarding home acted like they didn't know Geneva had children.

The four statements below "support" the main idea. Fill in the blanks with the correct word.

(a) Grace woke up feeling very _____ on Sunday morning.

(b) She was planning to strike up the _____ at dinner about why Geneva left forty-nine years ago.

(c) For months, since their _____ Grace had been looking forward to talking to Geneva about it.

(d) Grace excitement _____ when Geneva said that she wasn't going to dinner with them.

Story Elements: Dialogue
Read the following dialogues from Chapter 10 and write who said it.

"You all are early."   _____

"Do you want to sit where we were sitting yesterday?"   _____

"Geneva, I didn't know you had children!"   _____

"How do those feel?"   _____

"I am *her* daughter!"   _____

"Did you hear from Terrance?"   _____

"I'm not going!"   _____

Identifying Cause and Effect

"I went to the car and came back to the front of the house with the shopping bag in my hand. I took out the items and showed them to her. She tried on the shoes and said they were very comfortable. She really liked them a lot."

What is the Cause? _____

What is the Effect? _____

Reading for Information
Scan the text to find the answer for the question below.
What did Grace buy for Geneva while shopping in the city?

Contextual Meaning
Read the following line from Chapter 10 with the highlighted word and choose the best meaning for it.

"I couldn't help but marvel at the way she was **cognizant** about the time of day."

(a) unaware   (b) conscious   (c) ignorant

Character Trait Discussion
The Character Trait for Lesson Ten is "understanding".
Understanding means having sympathetic awareness or tolerance.

Read the statement below. Then choose <u>one</u> of the questions below and answer it. Write your answer in the space provided then discuss it with your group.

Although disappointed, Grace was understanding when her mother refused to go to dinner because of her hip problem.

1. How would you react if you made plans with someone and they backed out at the last minute?

2. Would you consider yourself an understanding person? Explain why or why not.

3. Do you think it is better to be understanding and not angry when someone does not cooperate with you? Why or why not?

Lesson Eleven - Worksheet

This lesson coincides with Chapter Eleven of the book, "After the Reunion: A Story of Acceptance". The purpose of this lesson is to analyze past events in order to understand the current situation in the story.
Chapter Eleven – "Day Four of Our Visit – Why Mother Left"

Main Idea and Supporting Details

Place an "X" on the line beside the "main idea" of the story.

_____ Grace felt nervous about asking her mother to talk about why she left.

_____ Grace's father never visited Geneva when she was put in a mental hospital.

_____ Grace was relieved that Arica's questions made Geneva talk about why she left.

The <u>four</u> statements below "support" the main idea. Fill in the blanks with the correct word.

(a) Geneva said that she was a _____ person when Grace asked her about why she left.
(b) Geneva totally _____ Grace's request to go outside and talk.
(c) Arica's plea had genuinely touched Geneva's _____.
(d) Geneva understood how _____ it was for her to open up and share her story.

Sequencing

Put the following dialogues from this chapter in the correct order.

_____ "I'm a private person."

_____ "I would come home on furlough."

_____ "I feel like I know. I just want to hear you say the actual words."

_____ "Yes, that's the same one,"

_____ "He was nice to me. He just wanted me to feel better."

_____ "Right. Well uh,"

_____ "Can she hear us?"

_____ "When we be on the phone, she eavesdrops and then she will gossip. So, I don't want to come right out with anything. You know?"

_____ "He and grandmother told me you left and you did not want me. But, even if that was the case, I forgive you."

_____ "Now or never."

Character Analysis
Describe Grace's psychological state when she tries to ask her mother to share her story about why she left forty-nine years ago.

Literary Elements: Theme
The Theme is the message that author wants to convey.

What is the theme of this selection?
(a) reunion　　　　　　　　　　(b) denial　　　　　　　　　　(c) rejection

Identifying Cause and Effect
"It all began before you were born. I would often feel tired from taking care of the five kids your father and I had together. He would go out of town for work, leaving me alone with them for one or two weeks at a time. I told him I needed a break from the kids…"

What is the Cause? _____

What is the Effect? _____

Interpreting and Evaluating Information
What kind of relationship did Geneva have with her husband?

Character Trait Discussion
The Character Trait for Lesson Eleven is "inquisitive".
Inquisitive means having or showing an interest in learning things.

Read the statement below. Then choose <u>one</u> of the questions below and answer it. Write your answer in the space provided then discuss it with your group.

Grace was very inquisitive in learning from Geneva the reason for her leaving.

1. What are some things you are inquisitive about right now? Explain why.

2. What would you do if someone was inquisitive about a secret you have kept for a long time?

3. Should one be inquisitive rather than mind their own business? Discuss.

Lesson Twelve - Worksheet

This lesson coincides with Chapter Twelve of the book, "After the Reunion: A Story of Acceptance". The purpose of this lesson is to analyze the author's feelings after visiting her mother.
Chapter Twelve – "Day Four of Our Visit – Returning Home"

Main Idea and Supporting Details
Place an "X" on the line beside the "main idea" of the story.

_____ Grace wishes that Geneva would agree to move to Kansas City.

_____ The trip had served its purpose for Grace as Geneva answered some questions.

_____ Geneva was perfectly happy with where she was staying.

The <u>four</u> statements below "support" the main idea. Fill in the blanks with the correct word.

(a) Grace did a lot of _____ about how she felt the visit had gone.

(b) She _____ her mother for doing the best she could to talk about why she left.

(c) Geneva was in _____ about a lot of the ways she was feeling back then.

(d) Grace _____ the things that Geneva felt comfortable sharing, but

_____ that she had truly given her all the facts.

Sequencing
Put the following dialogues in order from Chapter 12.

_____ "Wow, I am much prettier than I thought I was!"

_____ "Yes, I'm okay."

_____ "That sounds good!"

_____ "You only shared what you were comfortable with right?"

_____ "They don't read it!"

_____ "Miss. Geneva, this is heavy! How do you do it?"

_____ "Did you play the piano?"

_____ "I'm a strong woman, you just don't know!"

Literary Elements: Theme
What is the dominating theme in this chapter?

(a) rejection	(b) denial	**(c) reunion**

Figurative Language: Symbolism

Symbolism is anything that stands for something other than its literal meaning.
In the chapter, Geneva's "backpack" has been mentioned various times. Arica even says that it is very heavy. What do you think it symbolized?

Inference
What do you infer from the following line in Chapter 12?
"My heart wept for her at that moment."

Character Analysis
Analyze Geneva's character. She has been given three traits. Define those traits in your own words and quote evidences from the text.

Trait	Definition	Evidences
religious		
strong		
pretty		

Comparing and Contrasting
Compare Grace's feelings before and after the second trip.

Before	After

Character Trait Discussion

The Character Trait for Lesson Twelve is "accepting".
Accepting means taking or receiving something with approval or favor.

Read the statement below. Then choose one of the questions below and answer it. Write your answer in the space provided then discuss it with your group.

In this chapter, Grace is accepting the fact that her mother is happy staying where she is. She also accepts that Geneva left on her own accord.

1. Would you be accepting of someone who does something wrong to you?

2. Do you think it is better to be accepting and tolerant rather than impatient with others?

Why or why not?

3. Would you accept a loved one's wishes even if it did not make you happy? Why or why not?

_____
_____
_____
_____
_____
_____
_____
_____
_____
_____
_____
_____
_____

Book 4

Diary of Emotions

Answer Keys
30 Entries

Lesson One - Worksheet

This lesson coincides with a diary entry dated July 20, 2018 from "Diary of Emotions: Thoughts and Feelings". The purpose of this lesson is to analyze the main character's feelings and emotions after the main event took place.
Entry Date: July 20, 2018

Main Idea and Supporting Details
Place an "X" on the line beside the "main idea" of the story.

_____ Grace has accepted that her mother has a mental illness.

_____ Grace cannot understand how a mother can abandon her children.

_____ Grace wants to provide for and take care of her mother.

The <u>four</u> statements below "support" the main idea. Fill in the blanks with the correct word.

(a) Even though her mother left, Grace had completely _____ her.

(b) For years, Grace did not _____ her mother for leaving her and her siblings.

(c) I However, Grace finds it hard to _____ how a mother could not want to be close to her children.

(d) It hurts Grace that her mother has _____ to the point where she does not want her children.

Plot Analysis: Internal Conflict

In a story, an internal conflict is a battle taking place within the mind of a character. This is also referred to as the "man vs. self" conflict.

In this diary entry, we see Grace having an internal conflict regarding her mother. Which statement shows Grace's internal conflict? Circle the letter for the correct one.

(a) It is weird that my mother can leave me and I can still forgive her.
(b) A part of me wants to do things for her all the time, to take care of her.
(c) Still, I do not know how to feel about her.
(d) I know she was not capable of raising us….it still makes me want to accuse her of something.

Analyzing Characters and Incidents

In the boxes below, write three different lines from the diary entry that show Grace is saddened by her mother rejecting her.

```
┌─────────────────────────────────────────────────────────────┐
│                                                             │
└─────────────────────────────────────────────────────────────┘

┌─────────────────────────────────────────────────────────────┐
│                                                             │
└─────────────────────────────────────────────────────────────┘

┌─────────────────────────────────────────────────────────────┐
│                                                             │
└─────────────────────────────────────────────────────────────┘
```

Identifying Cause and Effect

"Seeing that she does not want to be with us, I feel like I should place some of the blame on her."

What is the Cause? _____

What is the Effect? _____

Drawing Conclusions

Read the following statement from the diary entry and choose the best conclusion for it.

"Like if I do not call her, we do not talk. If I stopped calling her, I would never hear from her again, even though she has my phone number. Then again, it may be for the best."

(a) Grace feels that her mother does not want to talk to her at all.

(b) Grace feels hurt that her mother does not get in touch on her own, but accepts it.

(c) Grace knows that her mother has a mental illness, but does not understand the reason for her mother's shyness.

(d) Grace is angry with her mother for not calling on her own even though she has their phone numbers.

Character Trait Discussion
The Character Trait for Lesson One is "forgiving".
Forgiving means being ready and willing to forgive.

Read the statement below. Then choose one of the questions below and answer it. Write your answer in the space provided then discuss it with your group.
In this diary entry, we see Grace's forgiving side as she says she had forgiven her mother for years.

1. Would you forgive someone who left you ages ago and reunited with them again? Why or why not?

2. Describe a situation where you had to forgive someone, or where you were the one seeking forgiveness.

3. Do you think it is difficult for some people to forgive? Why or why not.

_____

_____

_____

_____

_____

_____

_____

_____

_____

_____

_____

_____

Lesson Two - Worksheet

> This lesson coincides with a diary entry dated August 11, 2018 from "Diary of Emotions: Thoughts and Feelings". The purpose of this lesson is to understand the reason for the mother's attitude towards the main character.
> **Entry Date:** August 11, 2018

Main Idea and Supporting Details

Place an "X" on the line beside the "main idea" of the story.

_____ Grace wants to send her mother a few things, which will be useful for her.

_____ Grace wishes she could have a normal relationship with her mother.

_____ Grace feels hurt that her mother did not want to talk to her.

The four statements below "support" the main idea. Fill in the blanks with the correct word.

(a) It had been a few _____ since the last time Grace talked with her mother.

(b) Grace suspected that her mother had not been taking her _____.

(c) Grace assumed that her mother may not be _____ communicating with anybody.

(d) Grace understands that her mother is not _____ of doing anything for anyone.

Point of View: Objective vs. Subjective Narrator

*The **objective narrator** is a mere observer in the story and cannot enter into the minds of the other characters, except in a speculative way. This narrator is like a reporter on the scene of an event transpiring.*

*The **subjective narrator** on the other hand, knows everything about a single character and can see the story through the eyes of that character.*

Read the following statement and decide if the narrator is objective or subjective in nature.

I felt like maybe that might have been her way of saying, "Even though I enjoy these phone calls, I just do not care much for being on the phone."

(a) Objective point of view
(b) Subjective point of view

Making Inferences

An inference is an idea or conclusion that is taken from evidence and reasoning.
Based on your understanding of the text, answer the question below in a sentence or more.

How would you describe the relationship between Grace and her mother in this entry?

Analyzing Characters and Incidents

Circle the letter for the correct statement.

Why didn't Grace's mother want to come to the phone?

(a) She was probably actually busy with something.

(b) She did not feel like talking to anybody.

(c) Her hip was hurting badly.

(d) She was uncomfortable talking on the phone since she has been on her own for so long.

Identifying Cause and Effect

"I guess a part of me wants to support her in a bigger way, but when I call her and she says she does not feel like talking to anyone, well then, I feel like I should just let her have her life, you know?"

What is the Cause? _____

What is the Effect? _____

Character Trait Discussion

The Character Trait for Lesson Two is "understanding".
Understanding in this case means having sympathetic awareness or tolerance.

Read the statement below. Then choose one of the questions below and answer it. Write your answer in the space provided then discuss it with your group.

In this diary entry, Grace shows how understanding she is of her mother not wanting to talk to her by analyzing her feelings.

1. What are some ways in which you can show a person that you understand how they feel?

2. Describe a situation where your patience and understanding solved the problem.

3. Do you know someone who is tolerant with other people? Describe them.

_____

_____

_____

_____

_____

_____

_____

_____

_____

_____

_____

_____

_____

_____

Lesson Three - Worksheet

**This lesson coincides with a diary entry dated August 12, 2018 from "Diary of Emotions: Thoughts and Feelings". The purpose of this lesson is to identify some major themes in the text.
Entry Date: August 12, 2018**

Main Idea and Supporting Details
Place an "X" on the line beside the "main idea" of the story.

_____ Grace is confused about being responsible for her mother's care.
_____ Grace yearns to somehow take care of her mother and help her.
_____ Grace is thankful for her grandmother because she guided her properly.

The <u>four</u> statements below "support" the main idea. Fill in the blanks with the correct word.

(a) Grace wants to make sure her mother gets treatment for her _____ because she is always in pain.

(b) Grace looked online and found a _____ that her mother could use.

(c) Grace wishes to serve her mother _____ and oversee her _____.

(d) In addition to taking her out for walks, she wants to take her mother to the _____.

Literary Elements: Theme
In any literary work, the theme is the underlying message that the writer would like to get across. Circle all the themes that you can find in this diary entry.

(a) identity crisis

(b) longing for escape

(c) facing reality

(d) self-reliance

(e) acceptance

(f) rejection

Character Analysis

Read the following line from the entry and answer the question.

"Just thinking about my mother and a part of me says that is cool if she does not want to be with us, I haven't been with her all my life anyway. I know she has a mental illness, and that she is happy where she is. I feel like the biggest part of me does not really care. Then, there is that part of me that does care and that is the part of me that is talking right now."

Describe Grace's feelings in regard to her mother.

Identifying Cause and Effect

"I do not remember our utilities being turned off while my father was around. But, after he left us in the house alone, the utilities were disconnected due to nonpayment. I remember not having a phone even with my father around. I remember thinking, "When I grow up and get my own place, I am going to always have a phone, and my bills will always be paid."

What is the Cause? _____

What is the Effect? _____

Reading for Information

Grace mentions that if she retired and was home all day, she would invest in caring for her mother.

Scan through the text and list five things that Grace thought about doing with her mother.

(a) _____

(b) _____

(c) _____

(d) _____

(e) _____

Character Trait Discussion

The Character Trait for Lesson Three is "acceptance".
Acceptance means to leave something the way it is and not try to change it.

Read the statement below. Then choose one of the questions below and answer it. Write your answer in the space provided then discuss it with your group.

Grace accepts that because of her mother's condition, she cannot have a normal relationship with her.

1. Would you accept someone the way they are, or would you expect them to change? Explain.

2. Do you think it is important to accept others with their flaws? Why or why not?

3. How would you react if your friend was making fun of someone with a disability?

_____

_____

_____

_____

_____

Lesson Four - Worksheet

This lesson coincides with a diary entry dated August 22, 2018 from "Diary of Emotions: Thoughts and Feelings". The purpose of this lesson is to uncover important details to understand the situation of the characters.
Entry Date: August 22, 2018

Main Idea and Supporting Details
Place an "X" on the line beside the "main idea" of the story.

_____ Grace is eager to know more details about her mother's life.

_____ Grace feels bad for her mother not being able to have her family.

_____ Grace has a lot of admiration for her grandmother.

The <u>four</u> statements below "support" the main idea. Fill in the blanks with the correct word.

(a) From this entry, we learn that Grace's mother was adopted when she was _____ years old.

(b) Grace's mother was skilled at playing the _____.

(c) Grace's mother seemed _____ and did not worry about her relationship with her husband.

(d) Grace felt _____ in her father for putting his wife in a mental hospital and not visiting her.

Literary Elements: Theme
In any literary work, the theme is the underlying message that the writer would like to get across. Circle all the themes that you can find in this diary entry.

(a) betrayal
(b) individual vs. society
(c) love and sacrifice
(d) motherhood
(e) loss of innocence
(f) role of women

Literary Techniques

A literary technique is any method that the author uses to convey their message. Literary techniques are different from literary elements.

The following are some literary techniques:

Backstory: *This is a story that precedes the events in the story being told. This is some background information that adds meaning to current circumstances.*

Cliffhanger: *The story ends unsolved in order to interest the audience in a future episode for the resolution.*

Foreshadowing: *The author uses this technique to suggest events, which are yet to happen in the story.*

Look at the example from the diary entry and decide which literary technique the author has employed to convey her message.

"Now it all makes sense. I believe my grandmother did what she had to do in the situation. She could not have children of her own. She saw this cute little neglected girl, and took the steps necessary to have this little girl so she could take care of her."

(a) Backstory

(b) Cliffhanger

(c) Foreshadowing

Identifying Cause and Effect

"Finding her has just put a completely different view on the situation. I have peace, contentment, and comfort; and I feel empowered."

What is the Cause? Finding her has just put a completely different view on the situation.

What is the Effect? I have peace, contentment, and comfort; and I feel empowered.

Reading for Information
Scan through the entry to find the answers for the following questions:

How many years was Grace's mother married after she left Kansas City? _____

Name one or more things that Grandmother taught Grace's mother.

Character Trait Discussion
The Character Trait for Lesson Four is "curiosity".
Curiosity means a strong desire to know or learn something.

Read the statement below. Then choose one of the questions below and answer it. Write your answer in the space provided then discuss it with your group.

In this entry, we see Grace's thirst for information, as she wants to know more about her mother's youth and marriage to her father.

1. What is something you are curious about and why?

2. Do you think it is good to be curious? Why or why not?

3. What would you do if you could not get the information you needed?

_____

_____

_____

_____

_____

_____

_____

Lesson Five

This lesson coincides with a diary entry dated September 9, 2018 from "Diary of Emotions: Thoughts and Feelings". The purpose of this lesson is to understand the cause of the characters' feelings towards each other.
Entry Date: September 9, 2018

Main Idea and Supporting Details
Place an "X" on the line beside the "main idea" of the story.

_____ Grace hates to admit that her father was right about her mother.

_____ Grace is now okay with her mother not being in her life.

_____ Grace's mother just did not want any children.

The four statements below "support" the main idea. Fill in the blanks with the correct word.

(a) Grace's mother did not _____ her and her siblings when they got to her.

(b) She seems to be _____ without being in contact with Grace and her siblings.

(c) Grace feels _____ about her mother being okay without her.

(d) Grace believes that her mother left for a _____.

Literary Elements: Tone
The tone is the attitude of the author towards a subject or an audience.
Based on the lines below, decide on the tone for this entry.

"In all actuality, I pretty much feel the same way. Even though I am feeling emotional about this, there is still that part of me that feels like she has not been in my life for all of these years, so I am perfectly okay with her not being in my life now."

(a) amused

(b) resentful

(c) pragmatic

Identifying Cause and Effect

"So, I am in my feelings about the last time I called my mother and she said she did not feel like talking to anybody. This brings back memories of how my father would tell us that my mother probably would not receive us if we ever found her."

What is the Cause? _____

What is the Effect? _____

Interpreting and Evaluating Information

Based on your reading of the text, do you think Grace is still holding a grudge against her mother for abandoning her children? Explain your answer.

Character Trait Discussion
The Character Trait for Lesson Five is "adaptable".
Adaptable means being able to adjust to new conditions.

Read the statement below. Then choose <u>one</u> of the questions below and answer it. Write your answer in the space provided then discuss it with your group.

Grace shows adaptability in being okay with her mother not wanting to be with her.

1. Describe a situation where being adaptable will be advantageous to you.

2. Do you think being adaptable to new situations give you a better outlook in life?

   Explain why or why not?

3. Do you think change is good or bad? Discuss.

_____

_____

Lesson Six - Worksheet

This lesson coincides with a diary entry dated September 12, 2018 from "Diary of Emotions: Thoughts and Feelings". The purpose of this lesson is to understand observe some key events in the story to understand characters better.
Entry Date: September 12, 2018

Main Idea and Supporting Details
Place an "X" on the line beside the "main idea" of the story.

_____ Grace is thinking about furnishing her mother's room and buying her a phone.

_____ Grace's mother does not remember the memories that Grace shares with her.

_____ Grace is appreciative of her father for trying to keep the family together.

The <u>four</u> statements below "support" the main idea. Fill in the blanks with the correct word.

(a) Grace's mother volunteered in the _____ at the church they used to go to.

(b) She did not remember buying Grace _____ at the store.

(c) When she was a child, Grace would get into her mother's closet and put on her _____ and _____.

(d) She _____ being beaten by her husband and claimed that he treated her well.

Literary Elements: Style
In literature, style refers to the way the author uses words. It can include word choice, sentence structure, figurative language, mood, images and tone.

Here are some examples of styles in literature:

Expository: *This is mainly used for facts, educational information and is sometimes instructional in nature.*

Descriptive: *This style of writing includes a lot of descriptions. The author will use adjectives, adverbs, metaphors and sometimes poetic language to express their thoughts.*

Persuasive: *This style of writing targets a specific audience to persuade them towards a certain point of view. It presents an argument by presenting evidence to support an opinion.*

What style does the author employ for these diary entries?

(a) Expository

(b) Descriptive

(c) Persuasive

Identifying Cause and Effect

"I told her I remembered her laying in the grass in the backyard crying, afraid of being taken away. She did not really respond to that. Probably because it was a hurtful moment, and she preferred to talk about things that felt good to her."

What is the Cause? _____

What is the Effect? _____

Interpreting and Evaluating Information

Does the author feel more appreciative of her father in this entry?

Please expound on your answer.

Character Trait Discussion
The Character Trait for Lesson Six is "compassionate".
Compassionate means showing sympathy and concern for others.

Read the statement below. Then choose one of the questions below and answer it. Write your answer in the space provided then discuss it with your group.

Throughout the story, we have seen how compassionate Grace is with her mother despite the unexpected outcome. She even plans to provide a comfortable life for her mother.

1. Describe one instance where you were compassionate towards someone.

2. Do you think being compassionate all the time is a weakness? Discuss.

3. How would you deal with someone who treats people badly?

_____
_____
_____
_____
_____
_____
_____
_____
_____
_____
_____
_____

Lesson Seven - Worksheet

This lesson coincides with a diary entry dated September 15, 2018 from "Diary of Emotions: Thoughts and Feelings". The purpose of this lesson is elucidate lines from the text and analyze the emotions of the main character.
Entry Date: September 15, 2018

Main Idea and Supporting Details
Place an "X" on the line beside the "main idea" of the story.

_____ Grace has come to a realization that her mother actually does not want her.

_____ Grace's mother did not come to the phone because her hip was hurting.

_____ Grace only called her mother to check if she had received a package.

The <u>four</u> statements below "support" the main idea. Fill in the blanks with the correct word.

(a) Grace wondered if her mother was using her hip pain as an _____ to avoid coming to the phone.

(b) Grace feels almost temped to _____ trying to have an ongoing relationship with her mother.

(c) Grace's _____ and _____ told her that her mother did not want her.

(d) She finally accepts that they were telling the _____ about her mother.

Author's Purpose
Circle the letter for the correct answer.

What is the author trying to do for the reader in this diary entry?

(a) The author wants to <u>inform</u> the reader by teaching something.

(b) The author wants to <u>entertain</u> the reader by using something amusing.

(c) The author wants to <u>persuade</u> the reader to believe her point of view.

(d) The author wants to <u>create a mood</u> with descriptions to stir emotions in the reader.

Identifying Cause and Effect

"April said she would be sure to have her to call me tomorrow. We will see. Otherwise, I am almost tempted to give up trying to have an ongoing relationship with her."

What is the Cause? _____

What is the Effect? _____

Interpreting and Evaluating Information
What is the tone of the author in the following lines from the entry?

"I know she doesn't dislike me. She just never wanted so many children, and since she has been on her own for so long, she is happier that way."

(a) bitter

(b) benevolent

(c) aggrieved

(d) concerned

Character Trait Discussion
The Character Trait for Lesson Seven is "generous".
Generous means showing a readiness to give more of something.

Read the statement below. Then choose <u>one</u> of the questions below and answer it. Write your answer in the space provided then discuss it with your group.

Grace has shown generosity towards her mother in terms of affection and material things. In this entry, Grace calls the boarding home to check with her mother if she received something she sent her.

1. Name someone who you think is very generous and explain why.

2. How would being generous be advantageous to a person?

3. Describe any generous act that you did for someone.

_____

_____

Lesson Eight - Worksheet

This lesson coincides with a diary entry dated September 16, 2018 from "Diary of Emotions: Thoughts and Feelings". The purpose of this lesson is to be able to empathize with the main character and understand her conflict.
Entry Date: September 16, 2018

Main Idea and Supporting Details
Place an "X" on the line beside the "main idea" of the story.

_____ Grace is upset with her mother for not calling her about the package.

_____ Grace is having mixed feelings about continuing to keep in touch with her mother.

_____ Grace does not want to buy her mother more things because they could be stolen.

The four statements below "support" the main idea. Fill in the blanks with the correct word.

(a) Grace is considering not calling her mother again since she does not seem _____.

(b) Grace's mother said that she was in the hospital because she wanted a _____ from all of her children.

(c) Grace feels that she should simply be _____ with having found her mother before she passed away.

(d) Grace's mother has been living in a boarding home for _____ years.

Literary Elements: Conflict
Read the following lines from the entry and decide what sort of conflict Grace is battling.

"Well anyway, I have a decision to make. I have to decide if I am going to continue to try to reach out to her when it seems as if she does not really care about that. I feel torn between continuing to call her and stopping calling her. I guess I could talk to April about it first. April would probably say, "Just keep calling her," because she needs family even if she does not act as if she does."

(a) Person vs. Person   (b) Person vs. Self   (c) Person vs. Fate

Identifying Cause and Effect

"That could also be why neither he, nor my grandmother, took us to visit her in the mental hospital leading up to her disappearance. My father seemed to have known she would not receive us, so taking us to see her might have been more harmful for us than helpful."

What is the Cause? _____

What is the Effect? _____

Reading for Information
Scan through the entry to find the answers for the following questions. Answer them in a word or two.

(a) What desire did Geneva talk about during the therapy session? _____

(b) What is the name of Grace's daughter? _____

Interpreting and Evaluating Information
Read the following sentence and answer the question that follows.

"I guess my choice would be to know her, but I realize I am not going to have a mother in the way that I would like to."

Why do you think Grace prefers to know her mother despite the way she is?

(a) She does not want to enjoy the experience of having a mother.
(b) She spent so many years searching for her mother and wanting to know her.
(c) She wants to be able to take care of her and win her affection.

Character Trait Discussion
The Character Trait for Lesson Eight is "sensible".
Sensible means being practical and reasonable.

Read the statement below. Then choose <u>one</u> of the questions below and answer it. Write your answer in the space provided then discuss it with your group.

In this entry, Grace is sensible in analyzing her mother's condition and possible reasons for not talking to her. She even considers not sending her things because it would make her a target for the people living in the boarding home.

1. Do you think being sensible is better than being generous? Discuss with relevant examples.

2. Would you consider yourself a sensible decision maker? Explain why or why not.

3. Would you prefer to win a lot of money or go on vacation to a dream destination? Explain.

_____

_____

_____

_____

_____

_____

_____

_____

_____

_____

_____

_____

_____

_____

_____

_____

_____

Lesson Nine - Worksheet

This lesson coincides with a diary entry dated September 17, 2018 from "Diary of Emotions: Thoughts and Feelings". The purpose of this lesson is to understand the role of supporting characters in influencing the main conflict of the story.
Entry Date: September 17, 2018

Main Idea and Supporting Details
Place an "X" on the line beside the "main idea" of the story.

_____ Grace's father did not understand that her mother had a serious mental illness.

_____ Grace's sister has the exact same mental illness that her mother suffers from.

_____ Grace finally understands the struggles that her father underwent with her mother.

The <u>four</u> statements below "support" the main idea. Fill in the blanks with the correct word.

(a) Grace remembers that her father was _____ over her and her siblings.

(b) Grace realizes the _____ her father experienced just to keep the family together.

(c) Grace's father had gone through a lot trying to _____ children.

(d) Grace thought her father was making _____ when he was talking badly about her mother.

Making Inferences
Read the following line from the entry and answer the question.

"I never fully understood his anger and I never fully understood my father's commitment to us until I met and talked to my mother."

Why did it take so long for Grace to understand her father's commitment?

(a) She needed enough evidence from her siblings to prove that her father cared.

(b) She just needed time to think and analyze her father because she was too young.

(c) She needed to know her mother's side of the story before believing what her father said.

Character Analysis

Write 2 positive and 2 negative things about Grace's father in the table below.

Grace's Father	
Positives	**Negatives**
1.	1.
2.	2.

Identifying Cause and Effect

"It really made me feel some kind of a way that this worker knew my mother would be happy to see her son."

What is the Cause? _____

What is the Effect? _____

Character Trait Discussion

The Character Trait for Lesson Nine is "unprejudiced".
Unprejudiced means not having or showing unfair bias or prejudice.
Read the statement below. Then choose one of the questions below and answer it. Write your answer in the space provided then discuss it with your group.
Grace is unprejudiced when thinking about both her parents. She tries to understand the struggle faced by both of them, rather than judging quickly.

1. Do you think is it good to be unprejudiced in life? Why or why not?

2. Are you quick to judge people? How can you tell if someone is a nice person?

3. How would you deal with someone who misunderstood you and blamed you for something?

_____

_____

Lesson Ten - Worksheet

This lesson coincides with a diary entry dated September 30, 2018 from "Diary of Emotions: Thoughts and Feelings". The purpose of this lesson is to uncover more details about a specific character to understand them better.
Entry Date: September 30, 2018

Main Idea and Supporting Details
Place an "X" on the line beside the "main idea" of the story

_____ Grace appreciates her brother Jerome for sharing more details about her mother.

_____ Grace's mother, Geneva was skilled at doing things other than playing the piano.

_____ Grace's wants to move Geneva to Kansas City to buy her all of her favorite things.

The <u>four</u> statements below "support" the main idea. Fill in the blanks with the correct word.

(a) Geneva was good at doing things whenever she took her _____ properly.

(b) _____ and _____ told Grace about how talented her mother was.

(c) Jerome said that their mother's _____ was homemade and delicious.

(d) Grace wants to buy Geneva a _____ and a _____ if she moves to Kansas.

Reading for Information
Scan through the text and list four things that Geneva was good at doing.

1. _____
2. _____
3. _____
4. _____

Would Geneva still have all of her special talents today?

(a) Yes   (b) No

Identifying Cause and Effect

"Knowing those things that she is good at makes me want to bring her to Kansas City and get her involved in those things that she loves…"

What is the Cause? _____

What is the Effect? _____

Character Trait Discussion

The Character Trait for Lesson Ten is "talented".
Talented means having a natural aptitude or skill for something.

Read the statement below. Then choose <u>one</u> of the questions below and answer it. Write your answer in the space provided then discuss it with your group.

In this entry, we discover that Geneva had other talents besides playing the piano.

1. Name two or more of your talents? When did you discover you had them?

2. Have you ever made use of your talents to help someone? Explain how.

3. Describe an activity that you enjoy doing alone.

_____

_____

_____

_____

_____

_____

_____

_____

Lesson Eleven - Worksheet

This lesson coincides with a diary entry dated October 5, 2018 from "Diary of Emotions: Thoughts and Feelings". The purpose of this lesson is to identify the dilemma of the main character.
Entry Date: October 5, 2018

Main Idea and Supporting Details

Place an "X" on the line beside the "main idea" of the story.

_____ Grace wishes that she could have a normal relationship with her mother.
_____ Grace's accepts that her mother has a mental illness, but feels deprived of a relationship with her.
_____ Grace is happy she found her mother even if she has a mental illness.

The two statements below "support" the main idea. Fill in the blanks with the correct word.

(a) Grace tells us what it is like to be related to someone with a _____.

(b) She also says that accepting them like that does not take way the _____ of not having a normal relationship with them.

Making Inferences

"Sometimes, I wonder what is harder: living without a mother and not knowing her, or knowing her and having to live with the reality of her mental illness."

How do you think Grace is feeling about her mother in the lines above?

Character Trait Discussion

The Character Trait for Lesson Eleven is "perceptive".
Perceptive means having or showing sensitive insight.

Read the statement below. Then choose <u>one</u> of the questions below and answer it. Write your answer in the space provided then discuss it with your group.

In this entry, Grace is perceptive about the reality of being related to someone with a mental illness.

1. Do you consider yourself a perceptive person? Explain why or why not.

2. Do you know someone who is perceptive? If so, who? Please explain.

3. Do you think that being perceptive important? Why or why not?

_____

_____

_____

_____

_____

_____

_____

_____

_____

_____

_____

Lesson Twelve - Worksheet

This lesson coincides with a diary entry dated October 6, 2018 from "Diary of Emotions: Thoughts and Feelings". The purpose of this lesson is to understand the emotional impact of the situation on the main character.
Entry Date: October 6, 2018

Main Idea and Supporting Details
Place an "X" on the line beside the "main idea" of the story.

_____ Grace feels unwanted by her mother despite finding her after all these years.

_____ Grace's father left Grace and siblings alone while he worked in Florida.

_____ Grace is grateful that she finally found her mother and can do things for her.

The <u>four</u> statements below "support" the main idea. Fill in the blanks with the correct word.

(a) Grace feels _____ and _____ even though she found her mother.

(b) Geneva's story about why she didn't take her children with her, was _____ like how Grace expected it to be.

(c) Grace is disappointed with Geneva since she did not keep her _____ of calling her the next day.

(d) Grace is considering if it would be best to simply _____ from her mother.

Making Inferences

"I am happy to know she is in a stable place where she has been long-term, and she is not living on the streets. I can rest in the fact that this situation is the best it can be."

How does Grace feel about the situation with her mother in the lines above?

(a) She is happy that she has found her mother and need not care after this.
(b) She wants to accept that her mother is happy and lives in a stable place.
(c) She does not want to pressure her mother into moving to Kansas City.

Identifying Cause and Effect

"I believe it may have still been hard not having her at home. I would have likely felt responsible for her, starting at a very young age."

What is the Cause? _____

What is the Effect? _____

Character Decisions and Actions

There are many things in a story that can influence a character to take an action.

Even though Grace knows her mother does not want her, why does she continue to care for her mother?

Character Trait Discussion
The Character Trait for Lesson Twelve is "dutiful".
Dutiful means obediently fulfilling one's duty.
Read the statement below. Then choose one of the questions below and answer it. Write your answer in the space provided then discuss it with your group.
Grace is dutiful in the sense that she continues to fulfil the duties of a daughter to her mother.

1. Describe a situation where you were obligated to do something for someone.
2. What happens if you do not do something you are supposed to do?
3. Do you think it is better to be dutiful or not have responsibilities? Explain.

_____

_____

Lesson Thirteen - Worksheet

This lesson coincides with a diary entry dated October 8, 2018 from "Diary of Emotions: Thoughts and Feelings". The purpose of this lesson is to understand how the author copes with her situation.
Entry Date: October 8, 2018

Main Idea and Supporting Details
Place an "X" on the line beside the "main idea" of the story.

_____ Grace put all of her feelings about her mother into heartfelt poems and songs.

_____ Grace believes she has no reason to cry except for how unfortunate the situation is.

_____ Grace believes there is no reason to cry since her mother is taking care of herself.

The four statements below "support" the main idea. Fill in the blanks with the correct word.

(a) Grace thought that she would find her mother safe and secure in a _____.

(b) Grace feels that her mother is probably _____ than her.

(c) Grace is happy that her mother does not walk the _____ anymore.

(d) Grace now knows that her mother is strong enough to _____ of herself.

Reading for Information
Scan the text and find the answer for the following question.

According to the author's observations, what are Geneva's daily activities?

1. _____

2. _____

3. _____

4. _____

5. _____

6. _____

Identifying Cause and Effect

"She has been out there. She knows the streets. She was robbed on the streets. Now, she is afraid and I feel sad about that."

What is the Cause? _____

What is the Effect? _____

Interpreting and Evaluating Information

What do you think motivated Geneva to learn to take care of herself?

Character Trait Discussion
The Character Trait for Lesson Thirteen is "magnanimous".
Magnanimous means to be generous or forgiving.

Read the statement below. Then choose one of the questions below and answer it. Write your answer in the space provided then discuss it with your group.

Grace is magnanimous to her mother by understanding her struggle and caring for her. She has also forgiven her mother for leaving her so many years ago.

1. Describe how someone has been magnanimous to you.

2. Is it easy for you to forgive a person who did you wrong? Explain why or why not.

3. Would you forgive someone for what they did even if they do not change? Discuss.

Lesson Fourteen - Worksheet

This lesson coincides with a diary entry dated October 26, 2018 from "Diary of Emotions: Thoughts and Feelings". The purpose of this lesson is to observe the similarities the author has with her mother.
Entry Date: October 26, 2018

Main Idea and Supporting Details
Place an "X" on the line beside the "main idea" of the story.

_____ Grace cannot remember from whom she picked up certain traits and mannerisms.

_____ Grace's oldest sister Carla had picked up many things from their mother.

_____ Grace believes that she and her mother share some similarities.

The <u>four</u> statements below "support" the main idea. Fill in the blanks with the correct word.

(a) Grace has some _____ that are similar to her mother.

(b) They both say "_____!" in the exact same way.

(c) Grace has always said those words and so does her _____.

(d) _____ had probably picked up the saying from their mother as she was 8 years old.

Interpreting and Evaluating Information
Read the excerpt below and discuss the following two questions.

"Our "Oh, wow!" Is probably not hereditary. It is probably environmental."

How do you think Grace learned the saying "Oh, Wow!" when her mother was not around?
What is the difference between hereditary inheritance and environmental inheritance?

Character Trait Discussion

The Character Trait for Lesson Fourteen is "introspective".

The word **"introspective"** refers to someone who spends a lot of time examining their own thoughts and feelings.

Read the statement below. Then choose one of the questions below and answer it. Write your answer in the space provided then discuss it with your group.

Through this diary entry, the author is examining herself as to where and how she acquired certain characteristics. She is being introspective by analyzing her own traits and feelings.

1. Do you have a specific trait or mannerism that you inherited from someone? Discuss.

2. If you could change something about yourself, what would it be and why?

3. Do you think it is good to indulge in self-examination and exploration? Why or why not?

_____
_____
_____
_____
_____
_____
_____
_____
_____
_____
_____
_____

Lesson Fifteen - Worksheet

> This lesson coincides with a diary entry dated November 1, 2018 from "Diary of Emotions: Thoughts and Feelings". The purpose of this lesson is to understand the reason for the author not going ahead with a plan.
> **Entry Date:** November 1, 2018

Main Idea and Supporting Details

Place an "X" on the line beside the "main idea" of the story.

_____ Grace thinks it is important for her son, nieces and nephews to meet Geneva.

_____ Grace has thought many times about having her mother live with her.

_____ Grace is thinking about what could have happened if the wrong Geneva had come to the phone instead.

The four statements below "support" the main idea. Fill in the blanks with the correct word.

(a) At first, Grace thought that she would bring Geneva home so that all of her _____ would be able to meet her.

(b) The thought of moving to where Geneva lives, was only a _____ thought for Grace.

(c) Since Grace does not know Geneva too well, it would likely not be a good _____ for her to live with her.

(d) Grace does not see Geneva moving to where she lives as a real _____.

Making Inferences

Circle all of the reasons that Grace states for deciding not to have her mother live with her.

(a) She has given up on her mother being in her life.
(b) The boarding home takes care of all of Geneva's basic needs.
(c) Grace is still holding a grudge against Geneva for abandoning her.
(d) Geneva has been on her own for a very long time.
(e) Caring for Geneva may be a challenge since Grace does not know what her medical needs are.

Reading for Information

How did Grace know what Geneva sounded like when they spoke on the phone for the first time in years?

(a) She had always imagined what she would sound like for years.

(b) Her siblings had given her vivid descriptions of what she used to sound like.

(c) Her father would mock her mother's voice and she was able to recognize it on the phone.

(d) She had a recording of her mother's voice from a long time ago.

Identifying Cause and Effect

"She has been on her own for a very long time and, actually, so have I. It would probably be uncomfortable for us both."

What is the Cause? _____

What is the Effect? _____

Character Trait Discussion
The Character Trait for Lesson Fifteen is "rational".
Rational means basing an idea on clear thought and reason.

Read the statement below. Then choose <u>one</u> of the questions below and answer it. Write your answer in the space provided then discuss it with your group.

Grace is being rational in considering both the good and bad of having her mother live with her. It is only after careful analysis of the situation that she decides it is better her mother stays where she is.

1. What would happen if you let your emotions get in the way of rational decision-making?

2. Would you consider yourself a rational person? Explain why or why not.

3. Do you think rational thinking important in order to get through a difficult situation? Why or why not?

_____

_____

Lesson Sixteen - Worksheet

This lesson coincides with a diary entry dated November 20, 2018 from "Diary of Emotions: Thoughts and Feelings". The purpose of this lesson is to observe the difference in character decisions.
Entry Date: November 20, 2018

Main Idea and Supporting Details
Place an "X" on the line beside the "main idea" of the story.

_____ Geneva left on her own accord and not because of how her husband treated her.
_____ Grace's intention was to spend every moment with Geneva while they were visiting.
_____ Grace is thinking about the time she and her brothers went to reunite with Geneva.

The four statements below "support" the main idea. Fill in the blanks with the correct word.

(a) Grace and her brothers went back the next day to have a _____ dinner with Geneva.

(b) _____ declined the opportunity to go back.

(c) Grace intended to try to bring her mother home and build a _____ with her.

(d) Grace and Jerome had _____ intentions for their mother.

Character Decisions and Action
Grace and her older brother Jerome had different intentions when they reunited with their mother. Mention what they wanted to do in the table below.

Grace	Jerome

167

Character Trait Discussion

The Character Trait for Lesson Sixteen is "optimistic".
Optimistic means being hopeful and confident about the future.

Read the statement below. Then choose one of the questions below and answer it. Write your answer in the space provided then discuss it with your group.

In the story, we saw that Grace had been optimistic about reuniting with her mother and having her live with her in Kansas.

1. Does being optimistic always lead to a positive outcome? Discuss.

2. What are some things you are optimistic about, and why?

3. Why is the difference between and "optimistic" and an "opportunistic" person?

_____
_____
_____
_____
_____
_____
_____
_____
_____
_____
_____
_____

Lesson Seventeen - Worksheet

This lesson coincides with a diary entry dated November 22, 2018 from "Diary of Emotions: Thoughts and Feelings". The purpose of this lesson is to analyze the author's feeling about the kind of relationship she has with her mother.
Entry Date: November 22, 2018

Main Idea and Supporting Details
Place an "X" on the line beside the "main idea" of the story.

_____ Geneva confirmed that she had received the package that Grace sent her.
_____ Geneva wanted more yarn in order to knit a large men's sweater.
_____ After calling her mother, Grace had mixed feelings about sending her more things.

The four statements below "support" the main idea. Fill in the blanks with the correct word.

(a) Geneva liked the _____ and _____ that Grace had sent her.

(b) Grace felt _____ that someone had stolen the cod liver oil she sent Geneva.

(c) After the phone call, Grace ended up sending her some _____.

(d) Grace also felt _____ for not sending Geneva the additional yarn she wanted.

Making Inferences
Read the following line from the entry and answer the question.

"Thoughts of, "she should be living here with us," came to my mind. However, I know she is happy there. The thought of never sending anything there again also came to my mind."

Why do you think Grace was experiencing mixed feelings in this situation?

(a) Geneva had taken so long to confirm that she had received the package.

(b) Someone had stolen the cod liver oil that Grace sent for Geneva.

(c) She said that she needed more yarn for knitting a garment.

(d) There was no proof that Geneva was even using the things Grace was sending her.

Reading for Information

What are the two reasons for which Geneva had not begun using the knitting kit that Grace had sent her?

1. _____

2. _____

Character Trait Discussion
The Character Trait for Lesson Seventeen is "practical".
Practical means fitting the needs of a particular situation in a helpful way.

Read the statement below. Then choose <u>one</u> of the questions below and answer it. Write your answer in the space provided then discuss it with your group.

In this chapter, Grace is practical in not sending her mother the extra yarn that she needed because it might be stolen, or just not be used. By doing this, she is also lessening the burden for her mother in having to keep valuable things safe.

1. What other practical solution would you offer the author in this situation?

2. Do you think being practical can lead to misunderstandings in certain situations? Should that stop you from being practical?

3. Are you a practical person? Write three reasons to support your claim.

_____

_____

_____

_____

_____

_____

Lesson Eighteen - Worksheet

This lesson coincides with a diary entry dated December 1, 2018 from "Diary of Emotions: Thoughts and Feelings". The purpose of this lesson is to analyze the author's thoughts about some circumstances involving her mother.
Entry Date: December 1, 2018

Main Idea and Supporting Details
Place an "X" on the line beside the "main idea" of the story.

_____ Grace is thinking about moving Geneva to Kansas City soon.

_____ Grace is considering the possibility of them caring for Geneva when she can no longer take care of herself.

_____ Grace is not sure about what she would do if Geneva suddenly needed someone to take care of her.

The <u>three</u> statements below "support" the main idea. Fill in the blanks with the correct word.

(a) Grace is wondering what she would do if the _____ or _____ needed someone to care for Geneva.

(b) She is not sure if she should jump at the _____ to bring her mother close to her.

(c) Grace believes that her mother's _____ has controlled all of her decisions.

Making Inferences
Circle the letter for the correct statement.

How does Grace feel about when the time arrives for her mother to come live closer to her?

(a) She feels ready to take on the challenge of moving her mother to Kansas City.

(b) She is having mixed feelings and cannot tell what exactly she would do.

(c) She is thinking of how her mother might feel about living closer to them.

(d) She already has a plan for the time comes.

Character Trait Discussion
The Character Trait for Lesson Eighteen is "undecided".
Undecided means not having made a decision.

Read the statement below. Then choose one of the questions below and answer it. Write your answer in the space provided then discuss it with your group.

In this entry, Grace is undecided about what she would do when the time comes for someone to take care of her mother.

1. Describe a situation where you felt undecided about what you should do.

2. Do you think it is better to make decisions quickly in challenging situations or to take time?

3. Mention someone who is a good decision maker and explain why.

_____
_____
_____
_____
_____
_____
_____
_____
_____
_____
_____

Lesson Nineteen - Worksheet

This lesson coincides with a diary entry dated January 23, 2019 from "Diary of Emotions: Thoughts and Feelings". The purpose of this lesson is to study the conversation and analyze character feelings.
Entry Date: January 23, 2019

Main Idea and Supporting Details
Place an "X" on the line beside the "main idea" of the story.

_____ Grace called her mother after a few weeks had passed.
_____ Geneva informed Grace that she had received the box that she sent.
_____ Grace's grandmother always observed special occasions.

The four statements below "support" the main idea. Fill in the blanks with the correct word.

(a) When Grace called, Geneva came to the phone and was _____ to hear from her.

(b) Geneva asked if Grace had spoken to _____ and _____.

(c) Geneva's hip felt better since she got a _____ to help with the pain.

(d) Geneva reminded Grace that _____ was coming up.

Reading for Information
Scan the text and find the answers for the following questions.

1. How long had it been since Grace last called Geneva? _____

2. When did Grace send the box to Geneva? _____

3. What did grandmother do for Grace at bedtime? _____

Interpreting and Inferring
Read the following dialogue from the text and answer the question.

She said, "Thank you for calling. I like hearing your voice."
I said, "Thank you. I will try to call sooner next time."
She said, "Okay."

What can you tell about Geneva's feelings towards Grace based on her last response?

(a) She is genuinely happy to hear from Grace and wants to know more about her life.

(b) She is looking forward to Grace calling her again soon.

(c) She didn't care when Grace would call again, but was happy that she called when she did.

Character Trait Discussion
The Character Trait for Lesson Nineteen is "responsible".
Responsible in this sense means having care for someone as a part of one's role.

Read the statement below. Then choose one of the questions below and answer it. Write your answer in the space provided then discuss it with your group.

Even though she has mixed feelings, Grace feels responsible for her mother and calls her occasionally to check on her.

1. What is one of your biggest responsibilities? How do you feel about it?

2. Is being responsible a duty or something done by choice?

3. Do you think it is wrong to shirk your responsibilities? Why or why not?

_____

_____

_____

_____

Lesson Twenty - Worksheet

This lesson coincides with a diary entry dated April 20, 2019 from "Diary of Emotions: Thoughts and Feelings". The purpose of this lesson is to determine how characters will react to change.
Entry Date: April 20, 2019

Main Idea and Supporting Details

Place an "X" on the line beside the "main idea" of the story.

_____ Grace and her brothers showed Geneva a beautiful place to stay, but she declined.
_____ Geneva preferred to stay in the poor area where she is.
_____ Grace and her brothers have decided to let Geneva stay where she is.

The <u>four</u> statements below "support" the main idea. Fill in the blanks with the correct word.

(a) Geneva felt that Grace and her brothers were offering her _____ when Grace showed her the beautiful place.

(b) Grace feels that Geneva may not be _____ living in a community that was not poor.

(c) Grace wonders if Geneva would still need to carry her _____ around even if she lived in a place where nobody would steal from her.

(d) Geneva is _____ to live at the boarding home because it is her home.

Reading for Information

Scan the text and find the answer for the following question.

Why are the problems faced by Geneva at the boarding home?

Interpreting and Evaluating Information

Why does Geneva prefer to live at the boarding home and not close to Grace and her brothers?

(a) She is used to that way of life since she has been there for fifteen years.

(b) She knows the people there and they take care of her needs.

(c) She has been on her own for a long time and does not feel comfortable with her family.

(d) All of the above.

Character Trait Discussion
The Character Trait for Lesson Twenty is "self-reliant".
Self-reliant means being able to do things and make decisions by oneself.

Read the statement below. Then choose one of the questions below and answer it. Write your answer in the space provided then discuss it with your group.

Geneva is a self-reliant person, capable of taking care of herself. Since she has been on her own for long, she does not want to rely on someone else to provide for her entirely.

1. Do you think being self-reliant is better than depending on others for support? Discuss.
2. Is it good to be independent? How would an independent person solve their problems?
3. Are you a self-reliant person? Do others think you are? State your reasons.

_____

_____

_____

_____

_____

_____

_____

_____

Lesson Twenty-One - Worksheet

This lesson coincides with a diary entry dated April 20, 2019 from "Diary of Emotions: Thoughts and Feelings". The purpose of this lesson is to observe the author's decisions concerning her mother and determine if they are right or wrong.
Entry Date: April 20, 2019

Main Idea and Supporting Details

Place an "X" on the line beside the "main idea" of the story.

_____ Geneva has been getting strong medication for her hip problem.

_____ Geneva preferred another brand of cigarettes.

_____ Grace feels guilty about sending her mother cigarettes.

The <u>four</u> statements below "support" the main idea. Fill in the blanks with the correct word.

(a) Geneva told Grace that her favorite cigarettes were an _____ name brand cigarette.

(b) She said that she only smoked the affordable ones since she did not have _____ to buy the other brand.

(c) Grace does not feel comfortable sending her mother cigarettes because they are bad for her _____.

(d) She found out that it was against the law to send _____ through mail.

Character Decisions and Action

Although Grace feels guilty about sending cigarettes to her mother, she still considers it. Do you think she should have told her mother that it is bad for her, even if it was judgmental? Why or why not?

Write three things that Grace could send her mother instead of cigarettes.

1. _____
2. _____
3. _____

Identifying Cause and Effect

"I decided I would just send money instead. However, there are challenges to sending money because she does not have any way of cashing a check or a money order."

What is the Cause? _____

What is the Effect? _____

Character Trait Discussion

The Character Trait for Lesson Twenty-One is "thoughtful".
Thoughtful means showing consideration for the needs of other people.

Read the statement below. Then choose one of the questions below and answer it. Write your answer in the space provided then discuss it with your group.

Grace has been very thoughtful in getting Geneva whatever she needs even if it is cigarettes.

1. What is the most thoughtful thing someone has done for you?
2. Describe something thoughtful that you did for someone.
3. Would you buy someone the things they wanted even if it was harmful for them? Why or why not?

_____

_____

_____

Lesson Twenty-Two - Worksheet

This lesson coincides with a diary entry dated April 28, 2019 from "Diary of Emotions: Thoughts and Feelings". The purpose of this lesson is to observe changes in the author's mother.
Entry Date: April 28, 2019

Main Idea and Supporting Details
Place an "X" on the line beside the "main idea" of the story.

_____ Grace had sent Geneva some money to buy herself cigarettes.
_____ Geneva called Grace on her own for the first time.
_____ Grace has mixed feelings about Geneva calling her.

The <u>four</u> statements below "support" the main idea. Fill in the blanks with the correct word.

(a) Geneva _____ a call to Grace even though she had not called her first.

(b) She had called Grace _____ times in a row.

(c) She called to inform Grace that she had not _____ the money yet.

(d) The boarding home workers did not _____ Geneva to make the call.

Making Predictions

Grace has mixed feelings in regard to Geneva calling her for the first time on her own. However, she only called to inform Grace that had not got the money she sent her.

Do you think Geneva is beginning to get more comfortable with Grace? Do you think she would eventually be dependent on Grace and finally agree to move to Kansas City? State your reasons.

Character Trait Discussion
The Character Trait for Lesson Twenty-Two is "capable".
A **"capable"** person is someone who is able to do something effortlessly.

Read the statement below. Then choose one of the questions below and answer it. Write your answer in the space provided then discuss it with your group.
Grace never thought that Geneva was capable of initiating a phone call to her. Geneva has proved that she is capable of calling on her own too.

1. Name a few things that you can do effortlessly. Mention how long it took you to learn it.

2. Were you ever hesitant to try something new? Explain why.

3. How would a person find out if they are capable of doing something?

_____
_____
_____
_____
_____
_____
_____
_____
_____
_____
_____
_____

Lesson Twenty-Three - Worksheet

This lesson coincides with a diary entry dated May 12, 2019 from "Diary of Emotions: Thoughts and Feelings". The purpose of this lesson is to determine how the author's mother feels about not receiving something from her.
Entry Date: May 12, 2019

Main Idea and Supporting Details
Place an "X" on the line beside the "main idea" of the story.

_____ Geneva did not receive the money sent by Grace at all.
_____ Grace has decided not to send her mother anything for a while.
_____ Nobody answered the phone when Grace called the boarding home.

The <u>two</u> statements below "support" the main idea. Fill in the blanks with the correct word.

(a) Grace feels _____ because the money she sent never reached Geneva.

(b) She did not send a _____ for fear of it not reaching Geneva.

Making Predictions
How do you think Geneva is feeling since the money that Grace sent her never arrived?

Identifying Cause and Effect

"I am still feeling discouraged about the cash I sent last month never arriving, so I did not send a Mother's Day card for fear it would not reach her."

What is the Cause? Grace is feeling discouraged about the cash she sent never arriving.

What is the Effect? She did not send a Mother's Day card because she was worried that it would not arrive either.

Character Trait Discussion

The Character Trait for Lesson Twenty-Three is "giving".
Giving means to give something to someone voluntarily without expecting anything in return.

Read the statement below. Then choose one of the questions below and answer it. Write your answer in the space provided then discuss it with your group.

Grace has been very giving to her mother. She provides her mother with the things she wants even though she is not capable of doing anything for her.

1. Are you a giving person? Mention some nice things you have done.

2. It is better to be a giver or a receiver? Explain.

3. Describe something nice that someone has done for you.

_____

_____

_____

_____

_____

_____

_____

Lesson Twenty-Four - Worksheet

This lesson coincides with a diary entry dated May 13, 2019 from "Diary of Emotions: Thoughts and Feelings". The purpose of this lesson is to observe the result of the author's action.
Entry Date: May 13, 2019

Main Idea and Supporting Details
Place an "X" on the line beside the "main idea" of the story.

_____ Grace called her mother because she did not want her to feel like she forgot Mother's Day.

_____ Grace decided that she was not going to send anything for a while.

_____ Grace did not hear from her mother anymore since the cash got lost in the mail.

The two statements below "support" the main idea. Fill in the blanks with the correct word.

(a) Geneva did not come to the _____ when Grace called her on Mother's Day.

(b) A _____ at the boarding home did not bother with going and getting Geneva to talk to Grace.

Identifying Cause and Effect

"I have tried calling her since then, but she did not come to the phone. Therefore, after today, I may not be calling or sending anything for a while.

What is the Cause? I have tried calling her since then, but she did not come to the phone.

What is the Effect? after today, I may not be calling or sending anything for a while.

Character Trait Discussion
The Character Trait for Lesson Twenty-Three is "initiator".
An **initiator** is someone who begins something.

Read the statement below. Then choose one of the questions below and answer it. Write your answer in the space provided then discuss it with your group.
In this chapter, Grace is an initiator as she initiates a phone call to her mother on Mother's Day without being asked to do it.

1. Are you the one who initiates communication to your friends and loved ones? Explain how and when you do it.
2. Why is it important to be an initiator and not wait for someone to reach out to you first?
3. What would you do if you were in Grace's situation wherein you called to speak to someone and they didn't come to the phone?

_____

_____

_____

_____

_____

_____

_____

_____

_____

_____

Lesson Twenty-Five - Worksheet

This lesson coincides with a diary entry dated June 16, 2019 from "Diary of Emotions: Thoughts and Feelings". The purpose of this lesson is to understand the author's feelings about her mother's reaction to the situation.
Entry Date: June 16, 2019

Main Idea and Supporting Details

Place an "X" on the line beside the "main idea" of the story.

_____ Grace feels sad that her mother had not been coming to the phone.
_____ Grace is happy that she found her mother and knows where she is.
_____ Grace feels like the boarding home worker does not feel like getting Geneva to come to the phone.

The two statements below "support" the main idea. Fill in the blanks with the correct word.

(a) The boarding home worker told Grace that Geneva was in her _____.
(b) Grace was not sure if it was Geneva's own _____ to not come to the phone.

Interpreting and Evaluating Information

Write all the thoughts that could be going through Grace's mind about her mother in this entry.

Character Trait Discussion

The Character Trait for Lesson Twenty-Five is "complaisant".
Complaisant means willing to please others or to accept what they say or do without protest.

Read the statement below. Then choose <u>one</u> of the questions below and answer it. Write your answer in the space provided then discuss it with your group.

In this chapter, Grace is complaisant with her mother not coming to the phone despite her calling for the third time in a row to check on her. She finally accepts it and is just grateful for having found her.

1. Would you be complaisant with someone who does not want to talk to you? How?

2. Would you still be complaisant if someone was mean to you? State your reasons.

3. Do you think it is better to be complaisant to others, even if things don't go your way?

_____

_____

_____

_____

_____

_____

_____

Lesson Twenty-Six - Worksheet

This lesson coincides with a diary entry dated August 6, 2019 from "Diary of Emotions: Thoughts and Feelings". The purpose of this lesson is to observe the author's change in attitude towards her mother.
Entry Date: August 6, 2019

Main Idea and Supporting Details
Place an "X" on the line beside the "main idea" of the story.

_____ Grace feels sad about Geneva making excuses to get off the phone.

_____ Grace is wondering if she should continue to call her mother.

_____ Grace did not need to speak to Geneva when she called this time.

The four statements below "support" the main idea. Fill in the blanks with the correct word.

(a) Grace is undecided about whether or not she should continue to _____ communication with her mother.

(b) Grace had sent her mother a _____ package and called to check if it had arrived.

(c) Grace told the worker that she did not need to speak to her mother, but just wanted to _____ if she had received it.

(d) The truth about her mother making excuses to get off the phone was _____ for Grace.

Textual Evidence
From this entry, can you tell if Grace is putting some distance between herself and her mother? Pick two lines from the text to show this.

Character Trait Discussion

The Character Trait for Lesson Twenty-Six is "respectfulness".
Respectfulness in this case, refers to having a courteous regard for people's feelings and wishes.

Read the statement below. Then choose one of the questions below and answer it. Write your answer in the space provided then discuss it with your group.

Being respectful of Geneva's wish to not come to the phone, Grace asks the boarding home worker to check if she had received the care package.

1. How would you know if someone wants to be left alone?

2. Why is it important to be respectful to others?

3. Would being respectful help to earn you respect? Why or why not?

_____
_____
_____
_____
_____
_____
_____
_____
_____
_____
_____

Lesson Twenty-Seven - Worksheet

This lesson coincides with a diary entry dated September 15, 2019 from "Diary of Emotions: Thoughts and Feelings". The purpose of this lesson is to analyze the author's mother and identify the motive behind her actions.
Entry Date: September 15, 2019

Main Idea and Supporting Details

Place an "X" on the line beside the "main idea" of the story.

_____ Grace feels grateful to have found her mother and knowing where she is.

_____ Grace feels it would be best if she discontinues phoning her mother.

_____ Geneva does not really enjoy being on the phone.

The four statements below "support" the main idea. Fill in the blanks with the correct word.

(a) Grace does not feel like she should _____ her mother anymore.

(b) She will continue to call her mother only on _____.

(c) Geneva has been on her own for many years and Grace feels that she is _____.

(d) Geneva likes receiving gifts and mostly _____.

Analyzing Character

What are the four things that Grace has understood about her mother from her actions?

1. _____
2. _____
3. _____
4. _____

Making Inferences and Drawing Conclusions

Based on the entry, which statement about Geneva is most likely true?

(a) Geneva does not really want her family.

(b) Geneva prefers to be alone, even though she enjoys receiving things.

(c) Geneva does not care about hearing from Grace about her life.

(d) Geneva only cares about money and gifts.

Character Trait Discussion

The Character Trait for Lesson Twenty-Seven is "appreciative".
Appreciative means feeling or showing gratitude or pleasure.

Read the statement below. Then choose <u>one</u> of the questions below and answer it. Write your answer in the space provided then discuss it with your group.

Geneva is appreciative of Grace and her siblings caring for her even though she prefers to be alone.

1. Mention three things you are appreciative about right now, and explain why.

2. Do you think it is important to be appreciative of everything you have? Why or why not?

3. Have you ever been unappreciative of something until it went away? Explain.

_____

_____

_____

_____

_____

_____

_____

_____

_____

_____

_____

Lesson Twenty-Eight - Worksheet

This lesson coincides with a diary entry dated September 22, 2019 from "Diary of Emotions: Thoughts and Feelings". The purpose of this lesson is to understand the author's reason for discontinuing doing something.
Entry Date: September 22, 2019

Main Idea and Supporting Details
Place an "X" on the line beside the "main idea" of the story.

_____ Grace feels uncomfortable calling her mother.
_____ Grace sent her mother a small package just to acknowledge her.
_____ Grace really wants to know if Geneva had received the package.

The three statements below "support" the main idea. Fill in the blanks with the correct word.

(a) Grace feels that Geneva is _____ without her calling.

(b) Grace has to _____ with Geneva acting like she needs to get off the phone.

(c) Sending more packages would lead to Geneva carrying more items in her _____.

Making Inferences and Drawing Conclusions
Based on the entry, why is Grace most likely to stop calling and sending things to Geneva?

Circle the letter of all the statements that could be true.

(a) Grace feels that Geneva is far away and that makes it inconvenient.

(b) Geneva does not come to the phone when she calls.

(c) Although Geneva likes receiving things, Grace finds it challenging.

(d) Grace wants to treat Geneva the way she treats her.

(e) There is a risk of the package getting lost in the mail.

Identifying Cause and Effect

"If she stores it in her bedroom, it will be stolen.
Therefore, I have every reason to stop calling and to stop sending things."

What is the Cause? _____

What is the Effect? _____

Character Trait Discussion

The Character Trait for Lesson Twenty-Eight is "considerate".
Considerate means careful not to inconvenience or harm others.

Read the statement below. Then choose <u>one</u> of the questions below and answer it. Write your answer in the space provided then discuss it with your group.

Grace is considerate of Geneva and does not want to keep sending packages because she will have to keep carrying more things around.

1. Are you a considerate person? Mention some considerate things you have done.

2. Imagine you are planning to hold a party at your house with loud music, and there is a quiet elderly couple living next door. Would you still have the loud music?

3. Why is it important to be considerate to others and not always have your way?

_____

_____

_____

_____

_____

Lesson Twenty-Nine - Worksheet

This lesson coincides with a diary entry dated September 24, 2019 from "Diary of Emotions: Thoughts and Feelings". The purpose of this lesson is to understand the author's decision to stop doing something.
Entry Date: September 24, 2019

Main Idea and Supporting Details
Place an "X" on the line beside the "main idea" of the story

_____ When Grace called her mother, she actually came to the phone.
_____ The worker at the boarding home did not allow Geneva to speak for long.
_____ Grace has decided not to send her mother any more packages.

The three statements below "support" the main idea. Fill in the blanks with the correct word.

(a) Grace called Geneva to let her know that the _____ package she sent should have been delivered to her by now.

(b) Geneva informed Grace that the last package she sent her was stolen by her _____.

(c) Grace knew the type of _____ that Geneva lived in and still sent the package.

(d) This had become the _____ factor for Grace to not send Geneva any more packages.

Reading for Information
Scan the text and find answers for the following questions.

(a) How much time did the boarding home worker give
Geneva for using the phone? _____

(b) Did Grace spend a long time talking to Geneva on the phone?   Yes / No

(c) How did Grace feel when she overheard the boarding home
    worker speaking to Geneva? _____

Analyzing Dialogue

Analyzing the dialogue or conversation between characters is important as it helps to better understand the plot of the story.

Conversation
She began asking questions about how my day was going and what I had been doing. I answered, then, in turn, I asked her how she had been doing. She sounded like she was really enjoying me and that she was happy I called.

What does this conversation reveal about Grace's mother, Geneva?

Identifying Cause and Effect

She said, "My roommate stole it!"
I said, "That is horrible!" I saw it as a care package gone down the drain, but I could not blame anybody but myself.

What is the Cause? _____

What is the Effect? _____

Character Trait Discussion

The Character Trait for Lesson Twenty-Nine is "supportive".
Supportive means being helpful and providing encouragement.

Read the statement below. Then choose <u>one</u> of the questions below and answer it. Write your answer in the space provided then discuss it with your group.

Despite the situation with her mother, Grace is still supportive of her and does things in her best interest.

1. Who is the most supportive person in your life? Explain why.
2. Would you still be supportive of a close family member even if they do not offer you the same support?
3. Should you be supportive of your loved one even if they do something wrong? Why or why

not?

Lesson Thirty - Worksheet

This lesson coincides with a diary entry titled "In Closing" from "Diary of Emotions: Thoughts and Feelings". The purpose of this lesson is to understand the author's thoughts on reuniting with her mother.
Entry: In Closing

Main Idea and Supporting Details
Place an "X" on the line beside the "main idea" of the story.

_____ Grace has decided to stop calling Geneva to confirm if she received packages.

_____ Grace explains the many challenges faced by families after reunions.

_____ Grace has decided to let her mother call her instead.

The three statements below "support" the main idea. Fill in the blanks with the correct word.

(a) Grace says that people _____ that all family reunions end happily ever after.

(b) Witnesses never find out what _____ happened after the reunion.

(c) The _____ and _____ that Grace has experienced is nothing compared to finding her mother.

Reading for Information
Scan the text and find answers for the following questions.

What did Grace decide to send her mother instead of packages, and when?

Character Decisions and Action

What caused Grace to change her attitude in regard to communicating with her mother?

(a) It was challenging to call and send her things because she is far away.

(b) Whenever Grace sends her mother a package, there is a risk of it getting lost.

(c) Geneva never calls to confirm that she has received the package.

(e) All of the above.

Interpreting and Evaluating Information

How does Grace feel about her reunion with her mother? Does she regret it?

Character Trait Discussion
The Character Trait for Lesson Thirty is "charitable".
Charitable means relating to the assistance of those in need.

Read the statement below. Then choose <u>one</u> of the questions below and answer it. Write your answer in the space provided then discuss it with your group.

Grace has always been charitable to her mother by sending her things even if she didn't ask for them.

1. Describe a time when you gave something to someone who was in need?
2. Do you think being charitable is better than being a receiver? Why or why not?
3. Do you think being charitable is a weakness or a strength? Explain.

ABOUT THE AUTHOR

Dr. Grace LaJoy Henderson is the author of over thirty books. Her latest inspiration is the new Finding Mother Series of four books, in which Grace LaJoy shares her story of finding her mother who abandoned her after forty-nine years.

Her foster care story, *A Gifted Child in Foster Care: A Story of Resilience, Classroom Set* and her children's book series, *The Gracie Series*, are currently being used in public and charter schools. Pearson Higher Education published two chapters from her foster care story in a college textbook. Newspapers, radio and television have also featured her publications and her story.

She has earned a Doctorate in Christian Counseling, a Master's of Education in Guidance and Counseling, and a Master of Arts in Curriculum and Instruction. She has also earned a Bachelor's degree in Social Psychology.

Dr. Henderson managed a contract with the Missouri Children's Division, in which she provided court ordered mentoring for foster youth, supervised parent-child visits and parent education. She has served as psychology and college success instructor as well as academic coach. Outside of higher education, she is a keynote speaker, workshop leader and guest author at schools, libraries and other organizations.

Dr. Henderson is dedicated to educating and consulting with aspiring authors. She has conducted Young Author Workshops for secondary students.

Writer's Breakthrough:
Steps to Copyright and Publish Your Own Book

Do you desire to publish your own book?

Do you have a book ready for publication but do not know where to begin?

Writer's Breakthrough will teach you where to begin, guide you step-by-step, and help you publish your own book. ISBN: 978-0-9829404-4-0

www.gracelajoy.com

FINDING MOTHER SERIES – SECONDARY / ADULT

A collection of nonfiction stories from Grace LaJoy's own life. This inspiring series reveals how the author was abandoned by her mother, lived in foster care, and reunited with her mother after five decades; and details about what happened after the reunion. *Questions inspiring mental health discussion and reading comprehension are included in the back of each book.*

When Grace LaJoy published her foster care story, **A Gifted Child in Foster Care: Story of Resilience**, she thought she would *never* find her mother. But, she found her after 49 years! Now, she is sharing her fascinating story in an *inspiring book series you will love!*

ISBN: 978-1-7341868-0-2

Mother After Five Decades: A Story of Hope
Grace LaJoy's determination pays off when she finds her mother who abandoned her at age two. Discover the details of her intriguing journey in *Finding Mother after Five Decades*.
ISBN: 978-1-7341868-3-3

Reuniting with Mother: A Story of Tenacity
What happens when Grace LaJoy and her siblings come face-to-face with their estranged mother after 49 years? How does she receive them? Find out in *Reuniting with Mother*.
ISBN: 978-1-7341868-4-0

After the Reunion: A Story of Acceptance
After a very emotional reunion, Grace LaJoy has two concerns to address with her long-lost mother. What are her concerns? Does she get the answers she needs from her mother? Find out in *After the Reunion*. ISBN: 978-1-7341868-5-7

Diary of Emotions: Thoughts and Feelings
After reuniting with her mother after 49 years, Grace LaJoy toils with an array of thoughts and feelings. She reveals them all in *Diary of Emotions*. ISBN: 978-1-7341868-6-4

www.gracelajoy.com

A GIFTED CHILD IN FOSTER CARE – CLASSROOM SET

20 BOOKS, 20 STUDENT WORKBOOKS, 1 TEACHER'S GUIDE

ISBN: 978-1-7341868-0-2

A Gifted Child in Foster Care: *A Story of Resilience*
In this book, Dr. Grace LaJoy shares her life story of being deserted by her mother, living in foster care, and ending up in a gifted and talented class while still in foster care. She recalls her life story before, during and after foster care. Her turbulent life experiences reveal how she became strong and began to encourage, inspire and empower others through her gift of writing. Finally, she offers words of inspiration, encouragement, and empowerment to both children and parents. Children learn that they can succeed and impact the lives of others even in the face of adversity. Parents learn specific steps to help children recognize and utilize their gift(s). 5.5x8.5 112 Pages

ISBN: 978-1-7341868-1-9

A Gifted Child in Foster Care: *Student Workbook*
Reading Comprehension and Character Education for Students. This workbook for students will assist teachers in fulfilling the state requirements of the Grade-Level Expectations (GLE's) for Language Arts. The lessons will improve reading comprehension for students, while changing attitudes and building character. Students will read the chapters in the nonfiction book, A Gifted Child in Foster Care: A Story of Resilience – Revised Edition, individually or as a group. Then they will do the lessons from the workbook that coincides with each chapter. Teachers will be able to lead students in critical thinking exercises. Students will be able to develop and apply skills and strategies to comprehend, analyze and evaluate nonfiction. 8.25x11 64 pages. Teacher's Guide sold separately.

ISBN: 978-1-7341868-2-6

A Gifted Child in Foster Care: *Teacher's Guide*
Reading Comprehension and Character Education for Students. The Teacher's Guide contains the answers to the lesson activities in the Student Workbook, which is sold separately. It also contains additional lesson ideas that can be used in conjunction with the four core curriculum areas: Language Arts, Math, Science, Social Studies; also Career Preparatory and Communication Arts. In addition, it offers ideas about how to use "A Gifted Child in Foster Care" to teach more advanced reading comprehension skills. 8.25x11 68 pages.

Reading level grade 4+. Comprehension skills grades 4-7. Suggested for middle school students. However, high school students have been inspired by the author's story of resilience.

www.gracelajoy.com

THE GRACIE SERIES – ELEMENTARY (READABILITY GRADES 2 – 3)

The Gracie Series follows the lovable character Gracie as she gets caught up in funny situations. Parents, teachers and librarians will enjoy sharing these engaging stories and listening as the children share their thoughts sparked by the discussion questions in the back of each book. Each story was inspired by entertaining memories from the author's own life, teaching valuable life lessons while inspiring young readers to use reason, analyze and think critically. Your child will love these heart-warming stories and so will you!

ISBN: 978-0-9987117-0-6 Soft
ISBN: 978-0-9987117-1-3 Hard

Popcorn Behind the Bush
A delightful little mystery about a tin of popcorn. When Grandma sends popcorn in the mail and Gracie does not receive it, Gracie goes on a hunt to find out if her family members can help her decipher a note left by the Mailman. Gracie is just about to give up hope when she finally solves the mystery!

Cake in My Shoe
A very determined little girl. Gracie makes a promise to her father, but comes up with a plan to break it when she sees her brother doing something she wants to do.

ISBN: 978-0-9987117-2-0 Soft
ISBN: 978-0-9987117-7-5 Hard

Water in His Face
Gracie loves challenges! When Mother asks Gracie to help wake up Brother, she "jumps" at the challenge. But when her initial efforts to wake him does not work, she finally comes up with one last idea.

I Trimmed My Edges!
Grandma is coming over! When Gracie sees her family members making themselves look nice for Grandma, she wants to look nice for Grandma, too! What she does causes her family members to become outraged. But Grandma responds in a way that only a Grandma would.

ISBN: 978-0-9987117-6-8 Soft
ISBN: 978-0-692-89977-9 Hard

ISBN: 978-0-9987117-5-1 Soft
ISBN: 978-0-692-89959-5 Hard

Math on the Table
Two children excited about math, but only one math worksheet. When Gracie finds a mysterious math worksheet on the table, she goes on a quest to find out how it got there. When she is not able to find out who it belongs to, she makes a decision that causes her to learn a valuable lesson.

Puppy Ate My Shorts
A naughty little puppy takes a bite out of Gracie's new shorts two times. But after hearing wise words from Father, Gracie makes a different decision the third time around.

ISBN: 978-0-9987117-4-4 Soft
ISBN: 978-0-9987117-9-9 Hard

ISBN: 978-0-9987117-3-7 Soft
ISBN: 978-0-9987117-8-2 Hard

www.gracelajoy.com

MORE BOOKS BY DR. GRACE LAJOY HENDERSON

SECONDARY AND ADULTS

More Than Mere Words: *Poetry That Ministers*
Have you ever wished that someone could feel your Christian struggles and not be judgmental towards you? Have you ever needed just the right word at just the right time? Endorsed by Les Brown - author and motivational speaker, More Than Mere Words is a collection of powerful, spirit-filled, on-time messages. ISBN: 978-0-9747583-0-5

Love, Life and Relationships:
Poems from a Young Girl's Heart
Love, Life, and Relationships are poems written by Dr. Grace LaJoy, as a young girl, during the 1980's. The poems reveal her poetic thoughts about Love, Life, Friendship, Feelings, Hurt, Pain, Disappointment, Loneliness, Marriage, and Hope. ISBN: 978-0-9829404-8-8

Social Inspiration:
Christian Quotes for Life is a compilation of quotes written by Dr. Grace LaJoy's son, Aric J. Henderson during his four years in college. These quotes are a combination of Aric's creativity coupled with Godly wisdom and even a little humor. ISBN: 978-0-9829404-1-9

Unmerited Favor:
101 Quotes of Wisdom, Inspiration and God's Grace
A book of inspiring quotes written by Grace LaJoy Henderson.
ISBN: 978-0-9829404-6-4

www.gracelajoy.com

"Grace LaJoy Henderson's *Finding Mother Series* is a revelation. It is a gift to discover an author who can write so honestly—and with such vulnerability—about the joy and pain of reuniting with a parent after a 49-year separation. Henderson never glosses over the frightening or disappointing parts of her story. But her compassionate, unwavering voice, as she uncovers the long arc of her mother's life, is itself a triumph."
~Whitney Terrell, Associate Professor of English, University of Missouri-Kansas City

"The *Finding Mother Series* is a beautiful sequence of books. The author's reunion with her mother is very well documented."

~Phyllis Harris, Former Missouri State Director
Parent Information Resource Center

"The *Finding Mother Series* will inspire readers to *feel* their feelings. It stirs people in similar situations to be at peace, but at the same time seek growth, in the midst of their circumstances." Arica Miller, LMSW, School Social Worker

"The *Finding Mother Series* is a complex, touching opportunity for readers to see into the author's journey to find her mother after decades of searching. This series would be ideal for students at a secondary level who are searching for insight about the emotional conflicts and battles one must face when someone they care about has a mental illness. The four books in the series are segmented to provide specific lenses to the overall process, with a number of opportunities available for opening discussions about mental illness from both the author's point of view and her mother's." ~Leslie Arambula, M.A. in Creative Writing, English Teacher

"The *Finding Mother Series* displays a perfect example of how one triggering event can cause conflicting emotions. Throughout the series, the author experienced hope *and* despair, excitement *and* apprehension. Two, totally opposite emotions both at the same time. However, both were completely justified! This range and transition of emotions is what drives the entire series. Secondary students will absolutely benefit from reading this collection of books." ~Jacob Kelow, M.S.Ed., Secondary School Counselor, Kansas City Public Schools

"The author's emotional honesty and the balancing of positive and negative emotions is what makes this series work." ~Phoebe Shanahan, M.A. in English Literature

"The *Finding Mother Series* is written in a very powerful, real and authentic voice style. The author's honesty shines through her writing. Although the author's sadness throughout the story is quite palpable, her attitude towards her mentally ill mother is full of grace and understanding despite the fact that she had abandoned her. This is a clear and honest work."
~Fay Collins, Writer-Editor

Reducing stigma. Fostering connection. Inspiring hope.

www.ingramcontent.com/pod-product-compliance
Lightning Source LLC
Chambersburg PA
CBHW081228080526
44587CB00022B/3862